DOING CRITICAL ETHNOGRAPHY

JIM THOMAS
Northern Illinois University

Qualitative Research Methods
Volume 26

SAGE Publications
International Educational and Professional Publisher
Newbury Park   London   New Delhi

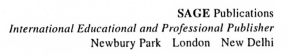

For information address:

SAGE Publications, Inc.
2455 Teller Road
Newbury Park, California 91320

SAGE Publications Ltd.
6 Bonhill Street
London EC2A 4PU
United Kingdom

SAGE Publications India Pvt. Ltd.
M-32 Market
Greater Kailash I
New Delhi 110 048 India

Printed in the United States of America

Library of Congress Cataloging-in-Publication Data

Thomas, Jim, 1941-
    Doing critical ethnography / Jim Thomas.
            p. cm. —(Qualitative research methods ; v. 26)
    Includes bibliographical references.
    ISBN 0-8039-3922-1 (cl). — ISBN 0-8039-3923-X (pb)
    1. Sociology—Methodology. 2. Ethnology—Methodology. I. Title.
II. Series.
HM24.T54   1993
301'.01—dc20   92-33062
                                                   CIP

93 94 95 96 10 9 8 7 6 5 4 3 2 1

Sage Production Editor: Tara S. Mead

CONTENTS

EDITORS' INTRODUCTION

The question of "What other?" is central in all qualitative research, because the other reflects back upon the self to which it is relevant or salient. Qualitative work involves in various degrees of intimacy the display of the self (the writer) and the other (the subject). The other is sometimes one's self seen from another perspective. This means that a shift in perspective means a shift in the other. Perhaps ethnography has the capacity to produce perspectives because, as Jim Thomas writes here, the culture of ethnography is a culture of people studying, writing about, thinking about, and talking to other people.

Critical ethnography emerges when members of a culture of ethnography become reflective and ask not only "What is this?" but also "What could this be?" Jim Thomas writes persuasively about how to sustain a critical perspective ("resisting domestication"), beginning to think critically, and implementing critical ethnographies, but he realizes his purpose best in his final chapter, in which he illustrates critical ethnography with his own studies of the social organization of prisons and "deviant" computer practices.

Thomas's analysis of violence is intimately reflective and shows how stereotypic racial thinking and practices are built into the social structure of the prison and how these, as captured in his analysis, reproduce racist practices among both people of color and others in the prison. Rather than seeing blacks as violent, Thomas argues that the white administrative and control structure (including job assignment and transfer practices) sustains racial divisions and racial violence, and that black gangs and violence are a response to these practices. Thomas cautions against facile studies, urges qualitative researchers to avoid traps, and shows how to do it.

The *other* of interest in this book is both the other of those not doing critical ethnography (how do they differ?) and the other of prisoners and hackers who represent society's view of them as violent, as criminals and deviants. Reflection on the symbolic meaning of these groups suggests that when one looks "back" one sees *how*, or the causes of these inequities, as well as "forward" to illuminate alternative courses of action.

—Peter K. Manning
John Van Maanen
Marc L. Miller

v

PREFACE

Critical ethnography is a way of applying a subversive worldview to the conventional logic of cultural inquiry. It does not stand in opposition to conventional ethnography. Rather, it offers a more direct style of thinking about the relationships among knowledge, society, and political action. The central premise is that one can be both scientific and critical, and that ethnographic description offers a powerful means of critiquing culture and the role of research within it.

Although the disciplinary influences here include anthropology, history, philosophy, and education, the sociological perspective dominates. This reflects in part my own training and current professional interests, and in part the greater body of ethnographic literature with which I am most familiar. However, I consider such disciplinary ruptures arbitrary—even violent—to the extent that one's intellectual tradition reflects administrative divisions and academic departments, rather than any necessary analytic boundary between core ideas and research practice.

Throughout, I have tried to convey that critical ethnography derives from a long tradition of social science, and I have included early practitioners liberally lest their legacy be forgotten. Collapsing an array of complex ideas into a short volume risks oversimplification; I have cited sources where ideas are developed more fully in order to encourage would-be critical researchers to begin developing an appreciation for eclecticism.

Writing projects are the product of a repertory cast of backstage critics, secondary contributors, supportive personae, and key grips. I am indebted to the entire ensemble, which includes John Van Maanen, Mitch Allen, Marc Miller, Phyllis Cunningham, Eleanor Godfrey, Al Futrell, Harry Mika, Jack Rhoads, Herbert Rubin, Kathleen Kemmerling, Jim Edwards, Fred Seymour, and Northern Illinois University's computer gurus, especially Vance Moore, Neal Rickert, and Joanne O'Donnell. Sharon Boehlefeld's assistance was typically invaluable. As usual, Peter Manning's suggestions and support exceed what can be acknowledged in a sentence.

DOING CRITICAL ETHNOGRAPHY

JIM THOMAS
Northern Illinois University

1. RESISTING DOMESTICATION

If the social doctors will mind their own business, we shall have no troubles but what belong to Nature. Those we will endure or combat as we can. What we desire is, that the friends of humanity should cease to add to them. . . . There might be developed a grand philosophy on the basis of minding one's own business. (Sumner, 1883, pp. 121-122; emphasis added)

Between consciousness and existence stand meanings and designs and communications which other men have passed on—first, in human speech itself, and later, by the management of symbols. (Mills, 1967, p. 405)

While an undergraduate at Michigan State University during the social unrest of the Vietnam War and civil rights struggles of the late 1960s, I took a course from a humanist social science professor who talked only about course content and refused to consider the relevance of the material to contemporary issues. During one of her lectures to the 500 or so students in the class, she held up a piece of chalk and asked, "What is this?" The responses varied: "chalk," "a writing implement," "an

1

elongated piece of white calcium carbonate." She was attempting to demonstrate how language and action combine to form meaning, and how labels are a powerful mechanism in limiting cognition. She was waiting for somebody to rise from his or her seat, take the chalk, and write on the blackboard as a means of demonstrating the *meaning* of the chalk.

To her pleasure, a future critical sociologist—one who had attempted to link course content to socially relevant issues—rose from his chair, slowly walked down the tier of steps to the dais, and gently removed the chalk from her hand. She seemed pleased that the "troublemaker" understood her point. But instead of walking to the blackboard, the student turned, gave the class a big grin, and then turned back to the professor and broke the chalk in half. He threw the chalk at her feet, raised his right hand with the middle finger extended, and whispered, "Fuck you!" He then returned to his seat. There appeared to be a conflict over meaning.

For the professor, the chalk's meaning was limited to a pedagogical technique and a means of communication that would be demonstrated by writing with it. For the student, the chalk more broadly signified frustration with the class and with an educational system that seemed irrelevant to contemporary problems. His performance translated into action the educational dissatisfaction for which the chalk stood. Breaking the chalk symbolized his reflection on the moral dimensions of pedagogy, the relationship between resistance and acquiescence to power and authority, and the relationship of knowledge to broader political questions. The chalk and the act of breaking it became an icon for the problems and issues of the times. Following sociologists before him, he began asking, "Knowledge for what?" (Lynd, 1939/1970), "Whose side are we on?" (Becker, 1967), "Why can't social scientists be partisans?" (Gouldner, 1968), and "Why should we be content to understand the world instead of trying to change it?" (K. Marx, 1846/1974, p. 123). He was no longer willing to follow Sumner's admonition to mind his own business. He was becoming critical.

Critical ethnography is a type of reflection that examines culture, knowledge, and action. It expands our horizons for choice and widens our experiential capacity to see, hear, and feel. It deepens and sharpens ethical commitments by forcing us to develop and act upon value commitments in the context of political agendas. Critical ethnographers describe, analyze, and open to scrutiny otherwise hidden agendas, power centers, and assumptions that inhibit, repress, and constrain. Critical scholarship requires that commonsense assumptions be questioned.

Most of us live in what Schutz (1972) calls a "taken for granted" reality, by which he means "that particular level of experience that presents itself as not in need of further analysis" (p. 74). This taken-for-granted world often seems too confusing, too powerful, or too mysterious to slice beneath appearances, and it is not always easy to see clearly, let alone address, the fundamental problems of social existence that we confront daily. Our culture entraps us in common sense and multiply segmented worlds in which "reality" includes a variety of mechanisms for assuring social harmony and conformity to interactional norms, organizational rules, institutional patterns, and ideological concepts (Berger & Luckmann, 1967, pp. 19-28, 53-55). Ritualistic social greetings can simultaneously invite others to interact with us or to maintain their distance; social roles provide cues for action while constraining or proscribing it; language both reveals and conceals; and even the most benign cultural symbols may possess potential threats. We create meanings and choose courses of action within the confines of generally accepted existing choices, but these choices often reflect hidden meanings and unrecognized consequences.

Conventional social science is one way to shed light on these problems. Some social scientists go a step further and engage in critical research that is explicitly political, yet rigorously scientific. Although not inherently better than conventional research, it provides insights about fundamental questions of social existence often ignored by other approaches.

Critical and Conventional Ethnography

Because ethnography traditionally has been associated with a potential critical mandate, distinct boundaries separating well-done ethnography from critical scholarship are often blurry. Critical ethnography is a style of analysis and discourse embedded within conventional ethnography. As a consequence, critical and conventional ethnographers share several fundamental characteristics. Among these are reliance on qualitative interpretation of data, core rules of ethnographic methods and analysis, adherence to a symbolic interactionist paradigm, and a preference for developing "grounded theory" (Glaser & Strauss, 1967). Nonetheless, several characteristics distinguish each from the other.

At its most general, *conventional ethnography* refers to the tradition of cultural description and analysis that displays meanings by interpreting meanings. *Critical ethnography* refers to the reflective process of choosing between conceptual alternatives and making value-laden judgments of meaning and method to challenge research, policy, and other forms of human activity (Thomas & O'Maolchatha, 1989, p. 147). Conventional ethnography describes what is; critical ethnography asks what could be.

Critical ethnography is not just criticism, which is a complaint we make when our eggs are too cold. Nor is it to be confused with critical theory (associated with the Frankfurt school), which is a theory of capitalist society. Critical ethnography is conventional ethnography with a political purpose.

Conventional ethnographers generally speak *for* their subjects, usually to an audience of other researchers. Critical ethnographers, by contrast, accept an added research task of raising their voice to speak *to* an audience *on behalf* of their subjects as a means of empowering them by giving more authority to the subjects' voice. As a consequence, critical ethnography proceeds from an explicit framework that, by modifying consciousness or invoking a call to action, attempts to use knowledge for social change. Conventional ethnographers study culture for the purpose of describing it; critical ethnographers do so to change it. Conventional ethnographers recognize the impossibility, even undesirability, of research free of normative and other biases, but believe that these biases are to be repressed. Critical ethnographers instead celebrate their normative and political position as a means of invoking social consciousness and societal change.

Critical ethnography is more than just the study of obviously oppressed or socially marginal groups, because researchers judge that all cultural members experience unnecessary repression to some extent. Critical ethnographers use their work to aid emancipatory goals or to negate the repressive influences that lead to unnecessary social domination of all groups. *Emancipation* refers to the process of separation from constraining modes of thinking or acting that limit perception of and action toward realizing alternative possibilities. *Repression* is the condition in which thought and action are constrained in ways that banish recognition of these alternatives. Critical ethnography is simultaneously hermeneutic and emancipatory.

Ethnographic *hermeneutics,* the science of understanding—or more accurately, of preventing misunderstanding—involves reducing the refraction of images distorted by conventional science's interpretive prism as we translate what we see from one set of cultural symbols (those of our research subjects) to another (those of our audience). Ethnographic emancipation, the act of cultural liberation, loosens the unrecognized symbolic constraints that restrict our perception, interpretation, discourse, and action. It alerts us that things are not always what they seem.

The survival of any society requires repression of some acts, including predatory behavior, or the imposition of social norms such as language. Not all constraints, however, are equally necessary or beneficial for social harmony and growth. Constraints that give some groups or individuals unfair advantage to the disadvantage of others, or social elements that automatically exclude some people from full participation in (and the benefits of) the resources commonly available to those more privileged (e.g., health care, education, or employment) are considered unnecessary. *Unnecessary social domination* exists when constraints are built into cultural and social life in ways that promote such inequality (Schroyer, 1975). The norms that distribute power in language use, shape deference or courtesy rituals, or determine the form and content of college courses are but a few ways that some people are able to dominate others in culturally acceptable ways.

Conventional ethnography assumes the status quo, affirms assumed meanings when others might exist, and seldom reveals the perspective of research subjects on the researcher. Studies of deviance, for example, look at the overt processes of interaction, typified by Luckenbill's (1986) fascinating account of male prostitutes, Becker's (1963) study of marijuana smokers, Ball's (1967) study of neutralizing strategies of presentation in an abortion clinic, or Goffman's (1979) analysis of gender and advertisements. As insightful as these and studies like them are, they fail to integrate their descriptions of cultural parts into an analysis of the whole that raises the critical implications of the descriptions. This failure subverts researchers' utility as human tools of knowledge, because simply stating the cultural context is not sufficient for understanding our topic.

Analysis must also penetrate to a further level, if it is not to leave us with an unfortunate dualism. For description and analysis on the level of institutions and culture tempt us to accept culture as a self-contained universe;

culture becomes another reified entity, like prices, social classes, money, society, the State, and similar objects of our current study. (Lynd, 1939/1970, p. 21)

AN EXAMPLE FROM PRISON CULTURE

As a way of distinguishing between critical and conventional ethnography, consider the following narrative (describing an assault on a correctional officer) taken from a 1986 interview I conducted with a prisoner:

> [This guard would] mess with guys, and then he'd say, "Go ahead and beat me." And one day, somebody came up to him and hit him with a pipe, he's got a plate in his head now, [laughs] and he was lying on the floor, and blood was gushing [laughs], and he was crying like a baby: "Please don't kill me, please don't kill me." He thought he was going to die right there.

In conventional interpretation, this becomes an example of the violent nature of prisoners or the vulnerability of prison staff to inmate attack. These meanings arise from the presuppositions that violence is wrong, that prisons and those confined in them are dangerous, or that prisoners have no right to resist what they perceive to be abusive staff conduct. Never has anyone with whom I have shared this snippet looked beyond the immediate imagery to ask how the guard might be "messing" with inmates, what other options for problem solving are available to prisoners, or what the function of violence in prisons might be. One could also ask how such matter-of-fact portrayals of depressing events shape the researcher's perception of the culture and the informants, a consequence that almost impelled Yablonsky (1969, pp. 112, 116) to terminate his study of hippies. These kinds of questions rarely are asked, and they are precisely the lines of inquiry that, when ignored, tend to reinforce existing social images of our subject. Critical ethnographers, seeking something more, attempt to connect the "meanings of the meanings" to broader structures of social power and control (Pfohl & Gordon, 1986).

Of all disciplines, ethnography perhaps is situated best to provide the tools for digging below mundane surface appearances of the cultural basis of violence and other forms of social existence to display a multiplicity of alternate meanings. Bourdieu (1991) reminds us that institutions of power lie behind behavior and cultural meanings that construct and limit choices, confer legitimacy, and guide our daily routine. This power is symbolic in that it relies on shared beliefs and ways of expressing those beliefs. Symbolic power is violent because it appropriates preferred meanings and represses alternatives (Bourdieu & Passeron, 1979, p. 4). Lefebvre (1971) refers to the consequences of the conflict between repression of alternatives and evasion of control as the "terrorism of everyday life" (p. 145), by which he means the hidden and abstract forms of subtle intimidation and domination on which social existence is built. Critical ethnographers *resist* symbolic power by displaying how it restricts alternative meanings that conceal the deeper levels of social life, create misunderstanding, and thwart action.

A Walk on the Wild Side

Resistance entails wildness. An appeal to our wild side invokes a call to reject inhibitions imposed by assumed meanings and to cultivate in their place the fiercely passionate and undomesticated side of our scholarly nature that challenges preconceived ideas. Wildness is that side of us that allows for recognizing the meaning of prison violence as more than simply bad guys "acting out," or for realizing that breaking chalk is a reasonable classroom option. The core of critical ethnography is the study of the process of domestication and social entrapment (Mills, 1970, pp. 3-4) by which we are made content with our life conditions. If, as Karl Marx (1846/1974, p. 37) says, we constantly make up domineering false conceptions about ourselves, about what we are, and about what we ought to be and then bow down before our creations, we therefore live in a partially illusory world. "Intellectual wilding" is resisting domestication by identifying these illusions and questioning their necessity.

IDEOLOGICAL DOMESTICATION

Ethnographers, like their sibling social science colleagues, are "frequently mired in sterile methodological debates, and seem to have lost sight, at least provisionally, of the real questions associated with understanding social life" (Aronowitz & Giroux, 1991, p. 143). This means that we have lost our original wildness. To borrow from Pollner (1991, pp. 375-376) in a related context, the potential for radical critique has been sacrificed to disciplinary preferences for expansion of empirical limits. There is an outer rim of practices and processes that constrains our research and how we talk about it, and most of us are too concerned with what lies within this narrow universe to examine how its rim is created and what lies beyond it. Our problem is that we are accustomed to our intellectual leash; we have become domesticated.

Domestication not only leads to a form of benign ignorance, but also absolves us from certain kinds of social responsibility: Racism and sexism are things other people engage in; crime is a problem for police rather than partly a structural problem; and solutions to problems are the domain of experts and government, not individuals. We have no sense of the big picture that we feel is painted by somebody else's cultural brush, because we are not taught a "critical consciousness" (Shor, 1980, p. 47). We live in a reasonably literate information society, but we lack full awareness of the symbolic sources and processes that shape our daily lives, interactions with others, language, expectations, leisure time, and other aspects of social existence. We are reminded continually of crime, poverty, war, homelessness, unemployment, and other social problems, and if we are lucky, they belong to somebody else. Researchers study "things" in isolation from their processes. We restrict observation to the internal character of a topic by naming what we see and imposing these names onto the data in the guise of objective analytic categories; by sanitizing our research of the pathos, oppression, or despair of the subjects; and by failing to explore the ironic and emancipatory potential of our research.

Conventional research is tamed, but at an intellectual cost. The practice of all social science includes not only norms for gathering and processing data, but tacit rules that define how the world is and should be. These rules and norms constitute a built-in ideology that gives a rather narrow focus of what is studied, and there is little inclination to move beyond.

An *ideology* is a shared set of fundamental beliefs, attitudes, and assumptions about the world that justify "what is." Because they provide the conceptual machinery for questions asked or not asked, for the data we gather or ignore, and for the interpretations we choose as relevant to the exclusion of those that are not, they are a fundamental preconscious component of research. Social ideologies provide a shared system of symbols that reduce conflict and function as a social control mechanism by providing a noncoercive social glue that helps keep things orderly. Conventional social science, ethnography included, tends not to resist the glue, which results in intellectual domestication. Critical scholars, a rather undomesticated lot, are committed to questioning what the glue binds.

Ideologies tame us by constructing advance meanings and justifications for our actions and the actions of others. Those attached to the legitimacy of social roles ("women belong in the home"), social policies ("affirmative action is reverse discrimination"), social sanctions ("punishment is necessary for social offenders"), and economic attitudes ("buy American") are a few examples. All thought and language is, at root, ideological. It is not that ideologies predetermine our culture and lives, but that we generally do not recognize the extent to which we are constrained socially by ideological predilections. The problem, therefore, is not so much that we adhere to a given set of ideological premises, but rather that we fail to recognize the distortion our ideological preferences produce in our everyday life.

UNLEASHING CRITIQUE

Reminiscent of Lynds's (1939/1970, pp. 202-250) ironic "outrageous hypotheses," *unleashing* connotes taking the risk of freeing ourselves from accepted interpretations, even if they are shocking. For example, Tax's (1970, p. 111) suggestion that members of a cannibalistic culture may have a right to eat each other raises the question of how, as researchers, we conceptualize and respond to practices that most persons consider repulsive. His conclusion is that even repulsive practices have no significant bearing on how researchers develop an understanding of the culture and its population. To understand any culture, he argues, we may have to begin by unchaining ourselves from our own assumptions and creating new ones that correspond to the meanings of our subjects.

Critical researchers begin from the premise that all cultural life is in constant tension between control and resistance. This tension is reflected in behavior, interaction rituals, normative systems, and social structure, all of which are visible in the rules, communication systems, and artifacts that constitute a given culture. Critical ethnography takes seemingly mundane events, even repulsive ones, and reproduces them in a way that exposes broader social processes of control, taming, power imbalance, and the symbolic mechanisms that impose one set of preferred meanings or behaviors over others.

Contemporary Ethnography:
A Culture-Studying Culture

Ethnographers commonly draw their data from direct observations in fieldwork, leading to the generally accepted view that ethnography is "a research process in which the anthropologist closely observes, records, and engages in the daily life of another culture—an experience labeled as the fieldwork method—and then writes accounts of this culture, emphasizing descriptive detail" (Marcus & Fischer, 1986, p. 18).

This definition, however, is somewhat limited by disciplinary imperialism and casts the meaning in the method rather than in the purposes of research as qualitative cultural description. Although most ethnographers gather data through systematic or participant observation, other techniques are also used to retrieve objective meanings from subjective cultural experience.

> Every single human expression represents something which is common to the many and therefore part of [the] objective mind. Every word or sentence, every gesture or form of politeness, every work of art and every historical deed are only understandable because the person expressing himself and the person who understands him are connected by something they have in common; the individual always experiences, thinks, acts, and also understands, in this common sphere. (Dilthey, 1927, p. 146)

The detailed cinematic descriptions of Fred Wiseman (e.g., *Meat*), Studs Terkel's (1974) interviews of working people, Thomas and Znaniecki's (1927) documentary analysis of Polish peasants, and the interpretation of television soap operas (Longhurst, 1987), clothes (Cahill, 1989; Davis, 1988), suicide notes (Jacobs, 1967), tattoos (Seaton, 1987), or the "menace of margarine" (Ball & Lilly, 1982) all rely on rich data sources. Therefore, a broader definition seems more appropriate:

> *Ethnography is a culture-studying culture.* It consists of a body of knowledge that includes research techniques, ethnographic theory, and hundreds of cultural descriptions. It seeks to build a systematic understanding of all human cultures from the perspective of those who have learned them. (Spradley, 1979, pp. 10-11; emphasis added)

This broader definition expands access points into culture by supplementing participant observation with additional data sources and strengthens the ability of researchers to bring different analytic approaches to bear on their topics. This expanded definition has emerged with the evolution of the ethnographic tradition.

Contemporary ethnographers in the United States trace their recent roots from the British anthropologists of the nineteenth century to the "Chicago irregulars" of the 1960s (Carey, 1975; Faris, 1970; Irwin, 1987; J. Lofland, 1987; L. Lofland, 1980; Thomas, 1983). The Chicago school of ethnography of the 1920s was both an ideological reaction to the growing prominence of positivism and an intellectual response to the neglected underclass of Chicago's "socially disorganized" urban areas. Early Chicago ethnographers, following Park's counsel (1967, pp. 3-32) that urban areas are a "living laboratory," focused on taxi-hall dancers (Cressey, 1932), slums (Zorbaugh, 1929), transition in ethnic ghettos (Wirth, 1928), hobos (N. Anderson, 1923), criminals (Shaw & McKay, 1929; Thrasher, 1927), and other socially marginal populations. They were critical for their time because they subverted the traditional value-laden view of cultural "difference" by shifting the research focus from one of individual or group pathology to one in which behaviors defined as odd by the dominant culture made "normal" sense to the subordinate participants.

The popularity of urban ethnography diminished with the rise of functionalism in the 1940s and the resurgence of positivism in the 1960s as "grand theory." The "sociology of correlates" led to university curricula, research topics, and a journal review process that squeezed ethnography out of the mainstream. Although a few still-classic ethnographic exemplars emerged in the post-World War II decades—including David Matza and Erving Goffman; the prison research of Donald Cressey, John Irwin, and Donald Clemmer; and the interactionists influenced by Herbert Blumer—it was not until the formation of the "Chicago Irregulars" in 1969 that a solid core of mutually-supportive scholars again aggressively and systematically pursued the ethnographic tradition and revitalized it as a viable methodology. Dissatisfied with the ontological (what there is in the world to know) and epistemological (how knowledge about our topic is possible) constraints of then-conventional research, this dynamic group laid the foundation for a vibrant and increasingly methodologically sophisticated program of interpretive urban ethnography (J. Lofland, 1987; Manning, 1987), and their influence continues in journals such as *Urban Life* (which they founded and is now known as the *Journal of Contemporary Ethnography*), and *Symbolic Interaction.*

WHAT IS CULTURE?

Culture generally refers to the totality of all learned social behavior of a given group; it provides the "systems of standards for perceiving, believing, evaluating, and acting" (Goodenough, 1981, p. 110) and the rules and symbols of interpretation and discourse. Culture also includes the material and symbolic artifacts of behavior—such as belief systems (i.e., religion), conceptual machinery for ordering social arrangements (i.e., ideology), and preexisting structural (i.e., formal organizations) and material (i.e., tools) attributes, or what Marx has called the means and mode of production—upon which cultural meanings are re-created and maintained.

> In crude relief, culture can be understood as a set of solutions devised by a group of people to meet specific problems posed by situations they face in common. . . . This notion of culture as a living, historical product of group problem solving allows an approach to cultural study that is applicable to any group, be it a society, a neighborhood, a family, a dance band, or an organization and its segments. (Van Maanen & Barley, 1985, p. 33)

Creating and maintaining a culture requires continuous individual or group processes of sustaining an identity through the coherence gained by a consistent aesthetic point of view, a moral conception of self, and a life-style that expresses those conceptions in one's immediate existence and tastes (Bell, 1976, p. 36). These behavioral expressions *signify* a variety of meanings. As signifiers, they reflect a type of code that can be interpreted semiotically, or as a sign system amenable to readings independent either of participants or of those imposed by the dominant culture.

Signs are the words, gestures, or artifacts that represent a meaning that one intends to transmit to an audience. Traffic lights, flags, winks, or loud voices connote and denote particular meanings (Barthes, 1983; Burke, 1989; Eco, 1979; Manning, 1988; Saussure, 1966). These meanings are called *symbolic* because they are shorthand representations that stand for something else. A *sign system* is a combination of signs that strings the meaning of individual signs together for a complex message. The meaning of signs occurs within a social context, and successful communication requires that both senders and receivers recognize the "vocabulary" and translation rules by which a sign system makes sense. These rules are called *codes*. Semiotics, the science of signs, sign systems, and codes, is a useful tool for cultural analysis.

> All aspects of culture possess a semiotic value, and the most taken-for-granted phenomena can function as signs: as elements in communication systems governed by semantic rules and codes which are not themselves directly apprehended in experience. These signs are, then, as opaque as the social relations which produce them and which they re-present. (Hebdige, 1982, p. 13)

Culture, then, is not simply the sum of individual behaviors. It also establishes the foundation for communicating meanings and the ways by which these meanings are reproduced and transmitted (Hoggart, 1971; Lyotard, 1988a). But these cultural meanings and their forms of transmission are conservative to the extent that they possess an inertia that preserves established characteristics resistant to change (Lynd, 1939/1970). The meanings include the historical processes that shape them, the directions in which they channel cognition and behavior of members, and the prepatterned means by which alternative ways of seeing, thinking, and acting are systematically constrained. Cultural conservatism contributes to repressive communication by concealing the characteristics of repression and, even when these are discovered, making change difficult.

Ideal Speech Acts and
Repressive Communication

Gover's *The One Hundred Dollar Misunderstanding* (1961) describes a series of amusing miscommunications that occur when a white college student and black prostitute each consistently misinterpret the meanings of the other. He, thinking she is sincerely attracted to him, cannot understand her obsession for his money. She, thinking he wants a mistress, cannot fathom his resistance to her attempts at an economic sexual arrangement. The ensuing confusion reflects more than a series of disastrous episodes. The cultural ambiguity of sexuality, male-female gender role conflict, interpersonal manipulation, economic inequality, and the power asymmetry underlying racial meanings combine to illustrate how communication can be distorted even when communicants speak the same basic language. Preexisting cultural meanings repress the ability of either party to avoid engaging in a power game, and the result is the creation of barriers to understanding and action.

All cultural experience requires an interpretive reading. Learning the proper rules for coding and decoding the meaning of messages entails developing a way not only for learning the language, but also for understanding the multiple contexts in which some languages are necessary, irrelevant, or risky.

In an ideal speech act, understanding is based on several cultural assumptions. Among the most important are the presumptions that the speaker and audience possess mutual competency (i.e., there are no private languages) and that there is no intent to deceive (Habermas, 1972; Mueller, 1972). In the real world, however, especially one in which deceptive manipulation of symbols offers a useful resource, these assumptions break down. In everyday life, deceit, private languages, veiled meanings, communicative incompetence, differing interpretive abilities, and other factors mediate how identity is formulated, culture is understood, and behavioral responses are chosen and implemented (Bok, 1983; Goffman, 1967; Katovich, 1988). The necessity to manipulate symbols to one's own advantage subverts "authentic communication" by requiring some successful messages to depend on equally successful deception or concealment of other agendas that inhibit understanding.

The goal of communication is coming to a mutually reciprocal understanding through the meaningful exchange of symbols, and *repressive communication* refers to obstructions either in symbol creation or exchange (Mueller, 1972). A glowering look intended to intimidate a weaker communicant may violate social norms, but the meaning of intimidation of the look may be clear to both the sender and the receiver. This would be considered repressive because it reflects a form of communication with the goal of establishing asymmetrical power and control. The message symbolizes domination, and the participants in the situation lack the freedom to explore a full range of alternative vocabularies, interpretive rules, or negotiated definitions.

Repression permeates social existence, and the conflict between repression/evasion and compulsion/adaptation characterizes everyday life (Lefebvre, 1971, p. 145). Women may never be sure of the motives of males who show them attention, students may never be sure if the reasons for a low grade are the real ones, and police generally assume that "everybody lies." These are culturally shaped examples of repressive communication.

> Implicit in "repressive communication" is the assumption that, although there exists no "true" knowledge in the sense that there are ultimate theories and concepts independent of time and space, there are at each point in societal development explanatory concepts and statements that are valid for the understanding of society and for the self-understanding of the individual. If, for reasons related to the structure of communication, it is not possible for groups and individuals to locate themselves in society and to articulate their interests, repressive communication occurs. If predefinitions are inherited from traditional ideologies and explanations are engendered by specific interest constellations, repressive elements enter communication since the generalizations and synthesis attained through these elements become inadequate or obsolete. (Mueller, 1972, p. 103)

A nondistorted communicative experience would require symmetry in which no communicants possess a culturally defined privileged position because of role, power imbalance, status, or other attributes that create an advantage concealing, expressing, or disputing the message of the other. The conservative characteristics of culture, however, militate against symmetry of power, knowledge, or skills, and the potential for distortion exists prior to any speech act, because interpretations are prepatterned in a variety of ways that prevent understanding. Critical ethnographers attempt to identify and illustrate the processes by which cultural repression occurs. They then step back and reflect on its possible sources and suggest ways to resist it.

Dilthey argued that interpretative sociology can be objective and that researchers can uncover the subjectivity of others and the historically shaped creations deriving from it (Rickman, 1961). Within this tradition, the ethnographic experience can be seen as the exploration of a common, meaningful cultural world conducted by drawing on intuitive styles of feeling, perception, and guesswork. From these collective meanings we begin to create an understanding of the culture from the point of view of the other. This activity makes use of clues, traces, gestures, and scraps of sense prior to the development of stable interpretations. These piecemeal forms of experience can be classified as aesthetic and divinatory (Clifford, 1988, p. 36). The researcher collects, categorizes, and patches together fields of synecdoches, or parts of the whole, which are then used to help understand the whole (Clifford,

1988, p. 38). This is illustrated by Horowitz's studies (1982, 1983) of the culture of young urban Chicano males in Chicago. She found that the concept of honor, seemingly a minor data concept, was profoundly important in understanding gangs' interaction and social life. Honor, a part of the divinatory whole, wove together seemingly unrelated attitudes and behaviors that otherwise appeared as scattered tiles in the cultural mosaic. The trick to critical ethnography is to select the divinatory concept that best organizes the data in ways that explore repressive meanings in a scientific way.

Ethnography as Science

In the past decade, ethnographers have honed the scientific basis of their data gathering and analysis (e.g., Agar, 1980, 1982; Denzin, 1978, 1989; Douglas, 1976; Gladwin, 1989; Hammersley, 1990, pp. 5-15; Kirk & Miller, 1986; Lincoln & Guba,1985; Noblit & Hare, 1988; Van Maanen, 1983, 1988), and there is no longer reason to doubt ethnography's scientific credentials. Ethnography, after all, respects the same basic rules of logic (laws of identity, contradiction, and excluded middle), replication, validity, reliability, theory construction, and other characteristics that separate science from other forms of knowledge. When done well, ethnography is as scientific and rigorous as quantitative social science or even the natural sciences. If a particular critical ethnographic study is not scientific, the problem lies with lapses of the researcher and not with the perspective.

"Science" is the process of systematic understanding in ways that are rigorous (logical), testable (verifiable/falsifiable), and evident (empirical). One gross misconception of the sciences is that methodological precision necessarily translates into more sophisticated research. More precise measuring instruments and statistical techniques do not make one discipline more scientific than another. The proper question is whether our data are *adequately* precise, and to become enamored with precision for its own sake becomes a fetish that often leads to intellectual onanism rather than to new understandings.

Although considered "subjective" because researchers attempt to display the viewpoint of those they study, ethnography is as objective as any science. Critics confuse reports on subjective phenomena with the objective reporting of those phenomena. Subjective ethnographic data do not mean "whatever the researcher thinks"; they mean objectively reporting on the subjectivity of our subjects. Objectivity, in this sense, does not mean the absence of bias or a researcher's perspective, or blindly accepting subjects' reported psychological state of mind. As Kirk and Miller (1986, p. 10) argue, objectivity simply means taking the intellectual risk of being proven demonstrably wrong.

All science is, at root, a metaphor in that our conceptual models and theories provide "as if" images that stand for the things they represent. The theatrical metaphor of dramaturgical analysis, the biotic metaphor of functionalists, and the conflict metaphor of Marxian scholars are each social constructs used to make more intelligible a "world out there." As a consequence, discourse is, as semioticians and postmodernists remind us, a type of language game (Lyotard, 1988b; Lyotard & Thebaud, 1985). The "scientific logic," rigor, and—unlike most other sciences—the laying out of the researchers' own potential intellectual intrusions (e.g., biases in the questions we ask, shaping of the research problem, or choice of analytic framing concepts) are sufficiently well established that ethnographers need not be defensive about the scientific status of their approach. It is neither more nor less scientific than the "hard" sciences. It is simply another language for being scientific, because science is a way of thinking and not simply a technique for data processing.

2. BEGINNING TO THINK CRITICALLY

This chapter shifts from an overview of the ethnographic enterprise to a summary of its critical substance. Critical thinking is a metaphor that provides a value orientation, and the conflict between value-laden research and the norms of "objective science" poses problems for all researchers. This conflict must be confronted, lest our "science" be reduced to little more than articulate opinions. Not all critical scholars proceed in the same manner, and the conclusion of this chapter summarizes how some researchers implement it.

The term *critical* describes both an activity and an ideology. As social activity, critical thinking implies a call to action that may range from modest rethinking of comfortable thoughts to more direct engagement that includes political activism. As ideology, critical thinking provides a shared body of principles about the relationship among knowledge, its consequences, and scholars' obligations to society. The goal of critical thinking, however, is not to create like-minded ideologues or to recreate the world in one's own image. Rather, it challenges the relationship between all forms of inquiry and the reality studied and sustained.

Critical thinking challenges "truth" in ways that subvert taken-for-granted ways of thinking. As social scientists, we have become adept at expanding empirical limits for other researchers, but the new "facts" rarely contribute to reflective judgments. They only provide the basis for further accumulation of more facts and the narrative theories to "explain" them. We lack—or avoid—the wisdom to apply our knowledge to our personal and political lives (Mills, 1970). Critical thinking addresses this failure by not assuming the reality of "facts" and by recognizing that revelation is not merely announcing, but is instead a juxtaposition of and dialogue about alternative images.

The roots of critical thought spread from a long tradition of intellectual rebellion in which rigorous examination of ideas and discourse constituted political challenge. Social critique, by definition, is radical. It implies an evaluative judgment of meaning and method in research, policy, and human activity. Critical thinking implies freedom by recognizing that social existence, including our knowledge of it, is not simply composed of givens imposed on us by powerful and mysterious forces. This recognition leads to the possibility of transcending existing social conditions. The act of critique implies that by thinking about and acting upon the world, we are able to change both our subjective interpretations and objective conditions. Freedom, as a component of critique, connects the emancipatory, normative, and evaluative features of critical thought.

> Freedom, first of all, implies that man is not totally encompassed and submerged in that which he *de facto* is. The norm, secondly, is a demand made with respect to the facts. Finally, the value is a special light which must be distinguished from the light provided by the fact. (Quant, 1967, p. 30)

Critical thought challenges ideational (symbolic) and structural conditions not of our making:

> Critical self-consciousness is the ability (stifled in some, developed in others) to discern in any "scheme of association," including those one finds attractive and compelling, the partisan aims it hides from view; and the claim is that as it performs this negative task, critical self-consciousness partici-

pates in the positive task of formulating schemes of associations (structures of thought and government) that are in the service not of a particular party but of all mankind. (Fish, 1989, p. 497)

Critique conveys *freedom* in that it acknowledges the capability to explore alternative meanings without constraint. It denotes *value* because it requires a discerning rational judgment in order to choose between conceptual and existential alternatives, and it suggests *norms* to guide both the discourse and interpretative activity of knowing.

Critical Ethnography as Metaphor

Critical ethnographers do not reject the canons of science; instead they challenge its central metaphors and the way they symbolize their objects. Among significant variations between conventional and critical models of science, the most profound is between their central metaphors, or ways of seeing: mechanism (predictable systems of operation) and organicism (process and integration), respectively (Pepper, 1948, p. 280). Different metaphors obviously produce different sets of images to study, because they de-emphasize differences by categorizing sameness in the objects they represent (Lodge, 1977: 75). For example, viewing a given behavior as a pathology in which the actor is *acted upon* by forces impelling a particular behavior gives us a dramatically different focus than viewing the behavior as meaningful *action* upon the world in which those behaviors might symbolize resistance.

The works of early social-disorganization ethnographers from the Chicago school (R. Cavan, 1928; Cressey, 1932; Thomas & Znaniecki, 1927) illustrate this metaphorical difference. Theories of crime at the turn of the century depicted an image of deviant behavior as the result of abnormalities of the offender. The resulting metaphors of individual pathology created an imagery of the criminal as "different" or "sick." Some ethnic groups, such as Italians and Irish, were perceived as more criminally inclined than others, because the areas in which they lived had proportionally higher crime rates. The pioneering work of Shaw and McKay (1929), however, suggested that the crime rates of these groups decreased as they moved from the impoverished urban areas where crime was heaviest into more genteel neighborhoods. Ethnographers from the Chicago school suggested that there was something about the poverty of cities that disrupted the social fabric of those areas. This disruption contributed to criminal activity by creating "socially disorganized" areas that possessed fewer informal mechanisms for social control. The metaphor of social disorganization produced radically different images of criminal activity, the criminal, and the social milieu in which crime occurred than did the medical metaphor of pathology, which focused on the individual. The social-disorganization metaphors depicted the social milieu, not the offender, as "sick."

All knowledge and concepts are metaphorical in that they provide icons and mapping techniques for interpreting and speaking about the social terrain. The contours of the social world depicted by theories provide ways of both seeing and moving about within it. Metaphors allow us to examine and discuss our objects from several perspectives by employing alternative sets of images. Metaphors do not reproduce mirrorlike representations of the objects they characterize. Instead, they give directions for finding the images that are intended to be associated with that thing (White, 1978, p. 91). They have a focus and a frame that suggests interpretive rules for assigning meaning to them and the language by which we name and pull together those meanings (Hawkes, 1972; Manning, 1983).

The *critical metaphor* refers to a fundamental image of the world from which illustrative analogues may be derived (Thomas & O'Maolchatha, 1989). As metaphor, critical ethnography directs attention to symbols of oppression by shifting and contrasting cultural images in ways that reveal subtle qualities of social control. The critical metaphor also provides hints for reconceptualizing behavior, values, or social institutions into meanings from which to "read off" deeper structural characteristics such as ideology, power, domination, and structural logic (Habermas, 1971). The label *critical ethnography* conveys a particular social imagery invoked by scholars, and it is this invocation of a particular style of creating images that places one within or outside of the critical ambit. When critical ethnography is understood as a metaphor rather than a theory, the debate between conventional and critical scholars is not over differing truth claims, but over the metaphoric images that drive knowledge production.

Critical thinking begins with the recognition that ideas possess a dual-edged capacity to both control and liberate, and adherents pursue knowledge by challenging conventional, taken-for-granted conceptions about the world and about how we think about it in order to move beyond "what is" to a state of "what could be." Because critical ethnography begins its scientific enterprise from a set of value-laden premises, however, the question for critical ethnographers is whether one can begin researching with a set of values without distorting the research process.

Confronting "Value-Free" Facts

To begin from a premise that social constraints exist and that research *should* be emancipatory and directed at those constraints is an explicitly value-laden position. The fact-value problem centers upon the distinction between scientific claims, which are produced by evidence and demonstration, and value claims, which are produced by rhetoric and reason.

Facts are those tidbits of knowledge that can be demonstrated to be true, such as "today is Monday" or "spaghetti does not grow on trees." Values refer to normative statements about an object, such as "Mondays are bad" or "spaghetti is good." For those adhering to strict separation between the two, we can say that roses are red or that the social status of women is less than that of men, but we cannot say, as a scientific claim, that roses are beautiful or that kindness is preferable to cruelty.

All knowledge ultimately reflects a set of norms and values about what is worth examining and how. Sometimes values are implicit in the questions we ask, in the operational definitions we use, or in how we conceptualize an act. For example, to study "deviance" is to begin with a definition of behavior with roots in social norms, not in science. Studies of prison management assume, for better or worse, that it is desirable that prison administrators, not prisoners, run the prisons. The penetration of values is unavoidable, and the solution is not to try to expunge them from research, but rather to identify them and assess their impact.

THE LEGACY OF MAX WEBER

Although Max Weber is considered a progenitor of conventional social science, his work contains significant insights—and cautions—for critical analysts. Weber's essays "Politics as a Vocation" and "Science as a Vocation" (1946) provide insights into the claim that critical research need not be tainted by passing "ought" statements off as facts. Weber contended that facts and values led to two fundamentally different kinds of statements. He argued for *value-neutral* research, a term whose meaning has often been twisted to mean that he believed that research is without bias or lacks application to ethical issues. By "value neutral," Weber simply meant that the researcher should approach the topic "neutrally" and not prejudge or impose meanings or interpretations. One can study prisons and demonstrate their debilitating effects on inmates, but one cannot conclude from these effects that we ought to abolish prisons because of the "scientific fact" that it is more noble to be humane than cruel.

This does not mean that Weber felt that scientists had no role to play in formulating and implementing values. Weber's concept of an "ethic of responsibility" allowed him to argue that scientists could have an impact on important social issues in the way they formulate topics, choose to analyze them, and apply the results. One could, for example, argue to abolish prisons by looking at the consequences of prison policies, conditions, and existence. If the findings clearly demonstrate their debilitating impact and ineffectiveness in meeting goals, research findings might develop alternative policies that could include abolition.

The lesson for critical ethnographers is profound, but not complicated: We let the data speak to us, we do not prejudge or impose our own preferred meanings, and we make sure that we do not say *is* when we mean *ought*. We are, however, fully free—Weber might say obligated—to select our topics and pursue lines of inquiry that raise "ought" questions. As scientists, we are simply forbidden to submit value judgments in place of facts or to leap to "ought" conclusions without a demonstrably cogent theoretical and empirical linkage. In short, we can think critically through reflexivity and by rethinking our work and its implications in iterative (i.e., repeated) versions of the research process, but we must always analyze empirically.

Variations on a Critical Theme

Although critical thinkers share a set of basic tenets and goals, their individual intellectual and ideological preferences branch out in several directions. This may seem confusing at first, but the confusion dissolves if we recognize that the critical label actually refers to a broad range of approaches, not all of which are compatible. One can utilize the perspective as political action, participatory research, applied policy research, or community organizing, or one can observe from the sidelines by critiquing and challenging culture and its symbols.

The categories below are hardly exhaustive (see Hammersley, 1991; Van Maanen, 1988, pp. 127-130), and they are not intended to provide clear lines of demarcation between critical and noncritical studies. The goal is simply to identify a few of the more common approaches within fairly cohesive bodies of literature that challenge conventional ideas or social arrangements. Although sometimes overlapping and not always distinct, they can be placed on an analytic continuum ranging from "armchair reflection" to direct political action.

POSTMODERNIST ETHNOGRAPHY

Postmodernism, a form of cultural critique that emphasizes the arbitrary nature of cultural signs and their codes, has implicit and explicit relevance for ethnographers (Cullum-Swan & Manning, 1992, p. 3). Postmodernists tend to be "armchair radicals" in that their critiques focus on changing ways of thinking rather than calling for action based on these changes. Postmodernism is a reaction against "cultural modernity" and is a "destruction" of the constraints of the present "maximum security society" (G. Marx, 1988) that attempts to gain control of an alternative future.

Postmodernism's starting point is a critique of the Enlightenment as a failed rationalist project which has run its time but which continues to encumber contemporary thought with illusions of a rational route to knowledge, a faith in science and in progress. The radical core of postmodernism lies in its mission of shedding the illusions of the Enlightenment. (Hunt, 1991, p. 81)

Postmodernists claim that modernism is dead. Modernism's characteristics include (a) belief in the power of reason and the accumulation of scientific knowledge capable of contributing to theoretical understanding; (b) belief in the value of centralized control, technological enhancement, and mass communication; (c) adherence to established norms of testing validity claims; (d) acceptance of the Kantian view of the possibility of establishing universalistic value statements; and (e) belief in the possibility of progressive social change. In response, postmodernists offer an ironic interpretation of the dominance of a master technocratic or scientific language that intrudes into realms once considered private, the politics of techno-society, and the sanctity of established civil and state authority.

Postmodernism is characterized not so much by a single definition as by a number of interrelated characteristics (Harvey, 1989). Among the most prominent are dissent for dissent's sake (Lyotard, 1988b), a stylistic promiscuity that mixes and matches metaphors and symbols to obtain contrasting meanings, and a playful parodying of standard meanings to show their irony (Featherstone, 1988, p. 203). *Ironic meanings* are alternatives to the literal meaning of a symbol or text that seem to convey a surprising or contradictory message. As a consequence, irony is a powerful wedge for splitting hidden meanings from the obvious ones. Postmodernist thought attempts to strip away the familiar social and perceptual coordinates that comfortably anchor our common sense meanings (Cullum-Swan & Manning, 1992, p. 2; Latimer, 1984, p. 121) and searches for new ways to make the unpresentable presentable by breaking down the barriers that keep the profane out of everyday life (Denzin, 1988, p. 471).

Deconstruction and Social Inquiry. Deconstruction derives from the prolific works of Jacques Derrida (1976, 1978, 1982), whose casual use of the term in a 1966 lecture (Kamuf, 1991, p. vii) named his project of separating the meaning of a text from the authority of its author. The approach became popular especially among literary critics in the 1970s, but only recently have social scientists begun to borrow and integrate the central ideas. Social deconstructionists invert hierarchies of power and authority and challenge the dominant features of social structure-as-text and the ways we study them. As a consequence, the field of study becomes a text of signs. The variable meanings, applications, and consequences of these signs within their specific context of cultural use become the analytic focal point.

Like postmodernists in general, ethnographers following the deconstructionist tradition are characterized by what Berman (1990, p. 4) in a related context calls "theoretical skepticism" toward language and other communicative symbols in which no meaning is fully fixed or exhaustively definable. For ethnographers, this leads to the goal of deciphering and overturning the master cultural narratives that convey subtexts of dominant meanings that lay beneath the primary ones.

> If postmodernism is about anything it is about the materiality of language
> as a dynamic force in the ritual social transformation of an indeterminate
> range of human possibilities into the restricted moral economy of a given

order of things in time. Does this make any sense to you as a reader? Whether it does or doesn't, I assume, is a matter of language. Language that keeps us at a distance; or language that brings us together in a certain way, while exiling (at least for the moment) other ways of interpretively making sense of and/or being in relation to each other. (Pfohl, 1991, p. 10)

Pfohl's (1990) ethnographic surrealism depicts a society that terrorizes but lacks a language to express the pain. Others offer a similar view in more conventional terms. Denzin (1988, 1990a, 1990b), for example, challenges the cultural images created by movies and other cultural media to decipher how the conservatism and violence of contemporary society are re-created symbolically. He prods his readers to look at the extraordinary in the mundane. The works of Manning (1986, 1988, 1989, 1991, in press-b) shift from analysis of T-shirt graphics to cultural violence and the ironic meaninglessness of the most meaningful of events —death—in order to illustrate how subtle forms of social oppression are reproduced. Seaton's observations (1987) of prisoners' tattoos lead to a self-interrogation in which she subverts the unity of a spectator's perceptions and the objects perceived. Cobb and Rifkin (1991) deconstruct mediation proceedings in the legal realm and find that their supposed neutrality subtly reproduces power relations that hide behind the rhetoric of "neutral" discourse. Perhaps the most useful resource for postmodernist ethnography comes from the British journal *Theory, Culture and Society,* which consistently publishes postmodernist and other critical cultural studies that illustrate the diversity of the perspective.

The critical potential of postmodernism lies in its subversion of conventional ways of thinking and its ability to force reexamination of what we think is real. A postmodernist-influenced ethnography must confront the centrality of media-created realities and the influence of information technologies that "store, transform, and subtly shape life chances in the postmodern world, and the relativity of perspectives" (Manning, in press-a).

Ironically, postmodernism carries a potentially nihilistic message of distrust of Enlightenment belief in social progress and the possibility of establishing universal values, which are central to contemporary critical thinking (Habermas, 1984, 1987). But, as Manning (personal communication, 1991) has reminded me, the central ideas of postmodernism should be confronted as a question about the organizing precepts in visualizing a society where neither industrial production nor nature constrain us as they once did. It is a vehicle for the projection of future fantasies, and its strength is in pointing out what we do not know.

PARTICIPATORY ETHNOGRAPHY

Argyris and Schon (1991, p. 85) argue that social scientists are faced with the dilemma of choosing between rigor or relevance. Guided by the commitment that the production of knowledge should be applied to problems in the research setting from which it comes, participant researchers opt for relevance and identify closely with the needs and concerns of their subjects, using diverse perspectives that attempt to reconcile action with inquiry. These include participatory action research, action research, and participatory research.[1] Each of these positions begins from a similar premise: Social scientists should reduce barriers that separate the products of research from the research subjects. Although the terms are sometimes used interchangeably, each of these perspectives possesses nuances that distinguish its tasks and goals from those of the others. They differ from each other primarily on the degree of participation by subjects in the research process itself (Karlsen, 1991, p. 143).

Participatory Action Research. Although not the originator of participatory action research (PAR), William Foote Whyte remains perhaps the best-known exemplar (Whyte, 1991). His study of Italian "corner boys" in *Street Corner Society* (Whyte, 1943) is notable not only for its political subtext, but for a substantial appendix reflecting on the biographical, ideological, and other baggage he brought into the field, as well as the impact of the subjects on Whyte himself.

In most conventional inquiry, researchers serve as experts in the design, implementation, and policy suggestions for research projects. PAR advocates, by contrast, proceed from the premise that "science is not achieved by distancing oneself from the world" and that when possible, researchers should defer to the input of the subjects in the belief that "it is possible to pursue both the truth and solutions to concrete problems simultaneously" (Whyte, Greenwood, & Lazes, 1991, p. 21).

Typical studies have focused on agricultural collectives, workplace relations, and employee-management relations in an attempt to define the needs of subordinates and others normally excluded from decision-making processes (Whyte, 1991). Because this variant rarely challenges existing power relations, but rather serves a mediating function between the powerful and the less powerful, it has been criticized by other critical scholars for ultimately perpetuating systems of control. If we view critical studies on a continuum rather than by some absolute standard of purity, however, PAR offers a way to redirect attention from those who wield power to those who bear its consequences.

Action Research. Action research (AR) differs from PAR in that researchers use their questions, puzzles, and findings to build descriptions and theories and then test them from within the research setting itself (Argyris & Schon, 1991, p. 86; Karlsen, 1991, p. 147). Outcomes are tested through "intervention experiments" in the field of study.

> For example, in testing whether there is housing discrimination, couples with different racial and ethnic backgrounds but with similar incomes try to rent apartments. Action researchers compare how often dominant-group and minority couples are shown apartments in choice locations and whether the minority couple is shown apartments only in minority neighborhoods. (Rubin and Rubin, 1991, p. 168)

Action anthropologists (e.g., Schleiser, 1974; Tax, 1970) illustrate how engagement of researchers in Native American populations can be committed to the goals and interpretations of the host populations. Alinsky's community-oriented research (1969) in Chicago in the 1940s provides a model for contemporary scholars seeking to integrate knowledge production with political empowerment. The recent work of Elden and Levin (1991) illustrates how they integrated problem solving with the goals of empowerment by a negotiation process that unified the subjects' needs with the requirements of scientific rigor. In their study of merchant shipping, Walton and Gaffney (1991, p. 124) describe how each stage of their project to promote organizational change within the industry was shaped both by the subjects and by the actions that the research generated, and Levine's study (1982) of the Love Canal pollution disaster also demonstrates the power of knowledge when applied to a community environmental crisis. Wagner and Cohen's description (1991) of empowerment of the homeless following mobilization for more resources also illustrates the utility of critical scholarship coupled to social action.

Participatory Research. Participatory research (PR), developed especially by adult educators, is explicitly radical. If Bourdieu and Passeron (1977, p. 4) are correct in arguing that pedagogic authority is the power to sanctify cultural meanings, then PR's opposition to the primacy of the researcher in establishing and guiding the research agenda challenges what Collins (1979) has called "credentialing" (p. 202) Credentialing is the practice of officially certifying competence, and those so certified are given more power and influence in imposing their own preferred view of the order of things on others. By removing the criterion of credentials as a passkey into the realm of inquiry, participatory researchers aim to eliminate the "property of positions" (p. 203) that allows researchers in conventional research to monopolize knowledge production because of their status. PR proceeds from an attempt to generalize a *process* of research instead of its outcome.

Influenced especially by Friere's theory of radical education as a means of social change in Third World countries, participatory researchers follow his adage that oppression is domesticating, but through reflection and action the world can be transformed (Friere, 1972, p. 36). In the United States, this has commonly taken the form of organizing and "re-awakening the weakest sections of our society" (Tandon, 1981, p. 23) in economically or socially depressed urban areas in ways that empower through literacy while simultaneously producing research that stimulates political action (Castellanos, 1985; Dearruda, 1990; Heaney, 1983). Other examples of integrating research, research subjects, and direct action include Maguire's application (1987) of PR to feminism, Smith's studies (1990) of police raids on gay baths and the management of AIDS in Toronto, and Davenport's analysis (1990) of grass-roots training for educational activism in low-income Chicago neighborhoods. Street's study (1992) of Australian nurses is an excellent example of how critical ethnography integrates empirical analysis, theoretical conceptualization, and critical insights. With subtle irony, she illustrates how those charged with healing others employ shared meanings to create a culture in which the power/knowledge relationship renders them powerless, oppressed, and vulnerable.

These variants challenge normal science in several action-oriented ways. They subvert the dominant scientific practice of creating neutral and abstract knowledge to be used by those with the power to control it. By incorporating research subjects to varying degrees as near equals in the projects, knowledge is transformed into a collective enterprise in which its production and use are to be shared by those who are its focus. Researchers also become active in confronting explicit problems that affect the lives of the subjects—as defined by the subjects—rather than remain passive recipients of "truth" that will be used to formulate policies by and in the interests of those external to the setting. Despite variation in the emphasis, each approach assumes the subjects are competent to shape methodological, theoretical, and practical outcomes.

Finally, each variant elicits a "sociological imagination" among research subjects by stimulating at the practical level theoretical understandings about conditions of existence and what can be done to change them. Practitioners take seriously C. Wright Mills's dictum (1967, pp. 530, 674; 1970, pp. 11-13) to transform "private troubles," those problems that affect individuals, into "public issues," those larger societal processes that contribute to the troubles. Sharing the power of knowledge production with subjects subverts the normal practice of knowledge and policy development as being the primary domain of researchers and policymakers.

Marxian-Oriented Approaches

The term *Marxian-oriented research* refers to studies that focus on the cultural underpinnings of concepts that include class, ideology, or the "capitalist state." Marxian approaches to critical cultural analysis can be traced to the anthropological works of Marx's contemporary, Lewis Henry Morgan, who traced the transformation of societies from one form of social system into another. His observations influenced Marx and especially Engels in their analysis of social change (Block, 1983, pp. 9-10). Marx and Engels used cultural anthropology to describe or confirm the operative principles they saw in the capitalist process and to search for examples of noncapitalist societies against which to compare their own social systems (Block, 1983, p. 15).

Marxian anthropologists recognize that cultural knowledge is the product of a combination of different social processes, including practical activity, ideology, rituals, and myths, and that these cannot be understood outside of the experience of political domination (Block, 1989, p. viii). The emphasis on structural factors that shape culture, however, has tended to shift the research focus of Marxian practitioners away from immersion within a particular group to one that looks through a lens providing a more distant view, such as critical theorists' focus on mass culture, neo-Marxists' analyses of the commodification of culture, or the relationship between social control and "deviant" cultures.

Calls for a radical anthropology (Hymes, 1974) have not led to a ground-swell response, but there remain sufficient impressive examples to illustrate how Marxian cultural studies might proceed (Nelson & Grossberg, 1988). Among these are Block's studies (1989) of myths and rituals in establishing power relations, Challiand's (1969) study of ideology embedded in North Vietnamese peasant culture that contributed to the peasants' resistance against foreign domination and imperialism, and the corpus of works by Godelier (e.g., 1972, 1978) in which he examines the class-based relationship between the material forces of a culture and the representations, ideas, and symbolic patterns necessary for any kind of activity to occur. Others are more subtle in nature, such as Russell's examination (1989) of the transformations of power and ritual resulting from economic changes in an Asian society, or Littlefield's description (1989) of the closing of a Native American school when it no longer met the needs of a changing capitalist economy.

Some of the better Marxian studies of culture are not usually recognized as ethnographies, in part because the subject matter tends to focus on social structure. These studies tend to focus on such topics as the role of the state in culture formation, ideology as a means of legitimizing forms of control, or class and class structure in creating or reinforcing stratification systems. Some of the better examples include Thompson's study (1975) of the shaping of early eighteenth-century English law in the dialectical clash between class and culture, Genovese's (1976) analysis of slave culture as a form of resistance and accommodation, and Jones's description (1976) of class structure and culture in Victorian England. In conceptualizing a critical practice for ethnography, Ganguly (1990) suggests that conventional ethnographic studies of colonialism recreate the discourse of racial and cultural differences in ways that reaffirm the hegemony of the colonizers over the colonized. Other examples include Beisel's study (1990) of the class politics of vice laws and culture in late nineteenth-century Philadelphia, Seed and Wolff's analysis (1984) of class and cultural formation in nineteenth-century England, Bowler and McBurney's description (1991) of the gentrification of New York's East Village, and Naples's examination (1991) of gender, labor, and contradictions in the welfare state. Ethnographic novels also provide insightful illustrations of class conflict, typified by Tressell's depiction (1914/1954) of U.S. working-class structure and Plunkett's portrayal (1971) of Irish class structure prior to the 1916 revolution.

Typical criminological studies focus on law or the legal process, including McBarnet's portrayal (1981) of how the conviction process and the ideology of law mediate internal contradictions and Balbus's description (1977) of how the legal processing of participants arrested in inner-city disturbances in the 1960s reflected the tension between the power of the state and the relative autonomy of law in maintaining cultural order. Diamond's study (1971) indicates that an expanded legal apparatus reflects the weakening of cultural bonds as society is progressively controlled by signals contained in law's symbolic meanings. Others, influenced by the Frankfurt school, attempt to combine existentialism and Marx's early writings as a way to illustrate how social activity such as law can be used to empower and give meaning to social existence (Milovanovic & Thomas, 1989).

Marxian ethnographies remain underrepresented in ethnographic literature, perhaps because the nature of Marxian theory makes an explicitly "Marxist" ethnography difficult. The basic structural concepts, such as the labor theory of value, the dynamics of class struggle, and the law of tendential decline of profit, are not readily amenable to close cultural observation. Some researchers have attempted this with success, as in Willis's study (1981) of the relationship between education and class, Bourdieu's use of Marxian concepts as a metaphor for the power of language, Andersen's study (1981) of class consciousness among professional women, Edin's analysis (1991) of contradictions in the welfare state and its clients, or Leal and Oliven's critique (1988) of the class basis of Brazilian soap operas. As these and other cultural analysts have shown, the heuristic value of a Marxian-oriented perspective for examining historical transformations, ideology, and the dialectic of cultural formation indicate that "revisionist" scholars who rework Marx's ideas and integrate them into other paradigms can produce exciting scholarship.

Conclusion

Critical researchers range on a continuum from those who adopt a few of its characteristics to those who avowedly attempt to incorporate all of them. Some critical approaches, such as participatory action research or action research, seek dramatic reforms without fundamental structural changes. Others, such as participatory research or Marxism, are avowedly radical to the extent that they advocate replacement of existing forms of social organization.

32

Even the most modest of these approaches contains a subversive element, because they advocate changes that are not merely cosmetic, but possess the potential for "nonreformist reforms" (Gortz, 1968) that lead to fundamental social change through seemingly modest increments. We can choose to challenge the symbolic edifice on which culture is based, as postmodernists do by critiquing the power of language as a form of social control, or we can take a more direct approach and define and tackle community problems (Rubin, 1987, pp. 40-42; Rubin & Rubin, 1991, pp. 165-170; Smith, 1990).

As action, critical ethnography can be implemented in a variety of ways. First, and most modest, changes in cognition resulting from new ways of thinking are an important step toward recognizing alternatives. Second, we should never underestimate the power of interaction with others as a form of action, because new ways of thinking can be contagious. Third, interaction can lead to networking, in which we unite with others for common goals, including conferences, writing projects, and action-oriented groups. Fourth, those who teach have the opportunity to integrate critical thinking into their curriculum—not to impose a "correct" line of thinking, but to help students examine the conditions of their existence from their own perspective, whatever it might be. Finally, critical thinking can contribute to community organizing, legislative reform, or policy formation.

For some scholars, critical ethnography must remain a Marxist ideology to justify the label *critical*. For others, a broader socialist or humanist ethos drives research. Despite differences, these basic approaches are unified by a style of thinking and writing that links the elements of cultural description to social organization, social structure, or action. We must always remember, however, that any demand for ideological unity subverts the central project of critique. Insistence on "correct" political thinking dissolves critique into a narrow mode of inquiry that limits thought and diminishes possibilities for theory and action.

NOTES

1. A fourth variant, action science, is not sufficiently distinguishable from action research to be considered separately here. A summary of the perspective can be found in Whyte (1991, p. 97) and Argyris and Schon (1991, p. 87).

3. IMPLEMENTING CRITICAL ETHNOGRAPHY

Once we understand the critical potential of ethnography and the basis of critical thinking, the next step involves identifying techniques to implement it. This chapter outlines a few of the ways that a researcher can begin thinking about and practicing critical research at various phases of a project. Like making a stew, doing critical ethnography is more than just the sum of its individual tasks. Not every component will be critical, nor will all critical parts be equal in value for explanation. In fact, some individual works may not be recognized as critical until we have read several of the author's pieces and view them as a whole. For example, Clegg's (1975) study of construction workers seems a fairly conventional analysis of power until placed in the context of his later Marxian framework (Clegg, 1979). Nonetheless, there are a number of research dimensions common to all cultural research that require attention from the beginning through the conclusion of a project. They serve as guideposts for continual examination of research and reflection on purpose. Points at which critical thinking can occur include *ontology, topic selection, method, data analysis and interpretation, discourse,* and *reflection.*

Ontology

Critical ethnography begins from the premise that the structure and content of culture make life unnecessarily more nasty, brutish, and short for some people. Women exercise less social power and receive fewer social rewards than men, the poor are disadvantaged socially for cultural as well as economic reasons, black urban males go to prison disproportionately more often and die younger than their white counterparts, and senior citizens, students, social control agents, and many other groups each confront problems that derive from their cultural position. This premise is not taken on faith. Critical ethnography is grounded empirically in explicit prior evidence of a variety of debilitating social conditions that provide the departure point for research. For example, differing rates of alcoholism, drug abuse, cancer, crime victimization, stress, school dropout, unemployment, suicide, domestic violence, divorce, and other well-documented problems alert critical thinkers that cultural forces may shape both the conditions and social responses that disadvantage some groups more than others.

Critical ethnographers begin from a view of "what is out there to know," or an *ontology,* that furnishes a set of images and metaphors in which various forms of social oppression constitute what is to be known. The things we normally believe to be "out there" come from uncritically accepted preconceived assumptions about the world. This acceptance creates the "outer rim" of processes and practices that constrains the possibilities of analysis. By remaining near the center, researchers are directed toward comfortable topics, concepts, and theories and lose sight of those processes that create both the rim and the internal spectacles that define it (Pollner, 1991, p. 376).

Van Maanen (1988) reminds us that most ethnography proceeds from a "realist narrative" entailing an "author-proclaimed description and something of an explanation" (p. 45) for the cultural practices observed. A realist ontology relies on the native's point of view, as filtered through the data collector's interpretative framework, to provide a detailed, "thick" description (Geertz, 1973, p. 7) that lets the natives "do the talking."

Borrowing from Lukacs (1971a), critical realism penetrates to the deeper levels of meaning that lie beneath superficial surface appearances.[1] Bodies of ideas, norms, and ideologies create meanings for constructing social subjects and concepts like "gender," "race," and "student." These and other roles and identities typify the invisible realm of meanings that stratify people and distribute power and resources in subtle ways. For critical thinkers, the ontological assumption is that there is something else there that will take us beneath the surface world of accepted appearances and reveal the darker, oppressive side of social life. Once we have decided to pursue that something, the next step is reducing it to a manageable topic.

Selecting a Critical Topic

Topic selection is hard work and complicated. Even for experienced ethnographers, choosing a precise, focused topic is one of the most frustrating parts of research. Contrary to what we read in methods texts, topic selection usually begins with only a vague idea of some broad question or issue. It may not be narrowed down until well into data gathering. Such a beginning is anathema for those who believe that a topic must be defined by a tight, tidy question that includes an interview schedule, an explicit list of potential interviewees, and a coherent research timetable created in advance. Sometimes this is a sound approach, but it is often an impractical, even impossible, ideal.

Critical ethnography is even more difficult, because the focus of attention often lies in areas at first glance unnoticeable and within data sources possessing mechanisms to conceal, rather than reveal, their secrets. How, for example, can we prepare in advance a precise set of interview questions to study leisure time activity in prisons if we are not initially aware of the extent of illegal substance use, homosexuality, loneliness, or the illicit ways of allocating power and resources? All ethnography possesses the potential for ad hoc restructuring of the initial topic. Critical ethnography is especially susceptible to the need for flexibility, because the questions that are most interesting may not be revealed until considerable background data emerges.

Critical research generally begins with a broad notion of a problem-laden empirical domain. One must never say, "I'm going to show that university culture is racist," or "I'm going to prove that Alcoholics Anonymous is repressive," because the data may show the opposite. One's prior assumptions can be wrong and still be illuminating, as one frustrated student discovered when she began by attempting to show how professors stifle student creativity. She "discovered" that both students and professors face constraints to creativity with roots in the educational culture that lie beyond the power of any single professor to overcome. Although it is legitimate to build upon a body of existing literature that draws empirically derived conclusions, these conclusions then become working guidelines rather than truths to be proven, and critical thinkers must always be ready to modify or change their beliefs and theories if the data require it. It cannot be emphasized enough that a scientist never, ever, sets out to gather data simply to prove a point, and we always must be prepared to change our views about a topic.

Students may say, "I want to study racism in fraternities," or "I'm a stewardess and want to study sexist passengers." This is generally appropriate if it is based on firsthand experience about events in an actual culture. In this preliminary stage, a concrete problem has been identified and the question is not to prove anything, but rather to see if it in fact exists. If it does, then the task is to illuminate how it occurs and is managed in a given culture. The trick is to find ways into the problem and reduce an infinite range of possible issues to a few manageable ones. There is no magic formula for resolving this preliminary dilemma of topic reduction, but the best general advice is to begin reading relevant literature and reflecting on how the ideas and concepts gained from the readings relate to initial field observations. Glaser and Strauss (1967, p. 37) caution against this, however, because they fear the possibility of contamination resulting from the importation of external ideas that may not pertain to the immediate study. Their warning is useful, and care should be taken to use existing literature as signposts rather than as a crutch.

The rule of thumb in selecting and focusing on a topic is that it must be both fun and something for which one has a passion. Ethnography is hard work and is arguably much more arduous and frustrating than surveys or other quantification methods. Once we embark on a project, it will be a part of us for a considerable time. An undergraduate project usually requires an entire semester, and for others it may be a multiyear endeavor. If we lack feeling for the project, the intensity required for successful data gathering, analysis, and writing will become an insufferable burden. Further, if we cynically complete a project in which we lose interest, the unpleasant aftertaste of research drudgery remains long after the research tasks are completed. A project that fails to stimulate our passion will ultimately become oppressively tortuous and depressively boring.

A second and equally important guideline in topic selection for all ethnographers is that a topic can be any slice of social existence, and data can be found almost everywhere. For example, David Maines's (1992) article on subway riding grew out of his curiosity about why people moved from car to car as they entered and departed the train. Systematically observing people walking up and down stairs can lead to an analysis of gender differences in movement, the control of social space, impression management of "embarrassment," and gender-based body language (S. Cavan, 1966; Goffman, 1959). The difference between critical and conventional ethnographic topic choice begins with a passion to investigate an injustice (e.g., racism); social control (language, norms, or cultural rules); power; stratification; or allocation of cultural rewards and resources to illustrate how cultural meanings constrain existence.

I can think of no topic that does not raise these or other relevant issues. The important thing to remember is that what we choose to study is simply a window into a broader scene. When done correctly, we gain new insights that we would not otherwise notice. It is fully appropriate to start with a general topic and simply ask, "I wonder what's there?"

It is not so much *what* we choose to study, but *how* we zoom in on aspects of the topic that distinguishes critical from noncritical research. It is not that the critical ethnographer selects subject matter that is different from other perspectives, but rather that the topic is framed in a way that mines the subject field more deeply.

Methods

Methodology, the techniques by which we collect our data, is not a neutral enterprise, and how we gather data can dramatically shape the critical potential of the project (Habermas, 1979, p. 25; Lukacs, 1971a, p. 4). There are several important interrelated points to remember when gathering data.

DATA SOURCES

Where and from whom we obtain data ultimately provides the meanings that shape the analysis. The task is to identify the best sources that bear most directly on the topic. It is crucial to identify the types of informants who are most likely to possess an "insider's knowledge" of the research domain, as did Yablonsky (1969), whose study of hippies would not otherwise have been possible. We must therefore decide what count as data, who is best able to provide the most *relevant* information, and what problems of access we might confront in obtaining it.

If we have not fully narrowed the topic, it may be difficult to decide what do or do not count as data. This underscores the importance of a preliminary literature review and reflecting on the most important broad issues as a way of excluding topics that will not be addressed. Another trick is to begin data collection by first selecting those sources to which one can return later if further information is needed, saving the "one-shot" sources for near the end, when the research questions presumably are better defined. For example, in my own study of prison culture, I had little idea of the direction the project would ultimately take. Therefore, I began simply by asking prisoners, staff, and administrators in casual conversations what they perceived to be the most difficult part of their prison experience. The theme of control and resistance emerged, and the most fascinating path for developing this theme seemed to be an examination of how prisoners managed the tension between resistance and accommodation to their existence. This provided the focus on prisoners, and by cultivating key informants, primary data sources were identified quickly.

If we want to study female deference to males in use of social space on subways, the most obvious way to obtain data is to ride the subways. If our observations are insufficient to explain what may seem to be inexplicable behaviors, however, we cannot change topics just because we are at an impasse or fatalistically conclude that some questions simply cannot be answered. The next step might be to devise a strategy to interview subway passengers, to conduct "distancing experiments" (e.g., breaching apparent spatial constraints), or even to draw from such analogous settings as buses, classrooms, or doctors' offices.

This, of course, holds true for all ethnography. For critical ethnographers the limits of relevant data may seem to close in much tighter and sooner, because we are looking at topics for which conventional native accounts may not always be sufficient when the answers are pre-patterned rhetoric that reflects learned accounts rather than actual reasons. When, for example, police officers consistently have a routine set of responses explaining how the impact of the Miranda rule hampers their work (despite research to the contrary), or when prisoners express in similar vocabulary why one must never express kindness in prisons (despite observations to the contrary), it is safe to assume that the rhetoric belies the reality, and standard means of probing are not sufficient.

Sometimes the gap between accounts and what the accounts describe is sufficiently interesting that the accounts themselves can become the focus of analysis. For example, Manning's (1980) study of drug agents illustrated how "narcs" have considerable disdain for drug users. Nonetheless, they must associate with them, cultivate their "friendship" if undercover or their loyalty when used as informants, and trust them for reliable information and testimony. The gap between onstage rhetoric and backstage action becomes a way of teasing out the contradictions that subjects must resolve when faced with competing demands of their daily existence.

The point to remember is that the data sources can include a person, a group, documents, or any other artifact that embodies cultural meanings. But although everything we see, hear, or stumble upon may become data, not all data are of equal quality or value. This means that we should continually be alert for additional sources of information that reveal the details and nuances of cultural meaning and process. "Trivial data" (Glaser & Strauss, 1967, p. 188), which are data from secondary analyses (e.g., surveys or quantitative studies) of our population done by others, can also be helpful in clarifying or verifying our own data. Glaser and Strauss cite the example of how a study of life-styles of social classes can be supplemented with market surveys. A student who is told by neighbors of a homeless shelter that "those people are always committing crimes" can check police reports, and a study of an athletic department's commitment to scholarship can draw from graduation rates and other studies of athletes' academic performance. Data are where you find them, and all things are potential data.

ACCURACY OF EVIDENCE

Glaser and Strauss (1967) repeatedly remind us that accuracy of evidence is, in their view, not as important for grounded theorists as for quantitative analysts:

> Even if some of our evidence is not entirely accurate this will not be too troublesome; for in generating theory it is not the fact upon which we stand, but the *conceptual category* (or a *conceptual property* of the category) that was generated from one fact, which then becomes merely one of a universe of many possible diverse indicators for, and data on, the concept. (p. 23)

This does not mean that we are not concerned with accuracy of evidence, or that we do not take great care to assure observational and reporting rigor. To ensure accuracy, the researcher must always constantly double-check interview and observational data for both accuracy and imposition of research values through leading questions or subtle misinterpretation that "confirms" some presupposition without actually demonstrating it. Experienced ethnographers recognize that when analyzing field notes, it is as important to analyze the interviewer's style of questioning and interjected responses as it is to interpret the responses themselves, because the interviewer's prompts can predetermine informants' discourse.

Critical ethnographers, like all other researchers, may publish a "wrong" or inaccurate account. There are several ways to minimize this. First, extreme care should be taken in observing, recording, and analyzing the data. Second, bringing to bear different data sources and gathering techniques on our evidence—what Denzin (1978) calls "triangulation"—enriches our evidence and often allows us to identify potential errors. Third, informants' or colleagues' readings of our drafts can be invaluable for spotting factual or conceptual errors. Fourth, replication of our studies by others illuminates the degree to which our evidence was accurate and our concepts fruitful. Finally, our own reflection on the study, even in hindsight, can suggest possible weaknesses that allow revision of the original study or strengthening of future ones.

DATA COLLECTION

Once we identify a few possible fruitful sources, collecting the data can offer opportunities for critical insights. As with all ethnographic research, the critical thinker should be alert for informant answers that are contradictory, that do not correspond to other informants' answers, that defy observed reality or that indicate cover-ups or gaps. Pursuing such anomalies is hard work, and the temptation to let them pass must be fought. When pursued, however, anomalies often lead to surprising information, and one of the greatest skills of an ethnographic interviewer is the ability to be prepared to identify and pursue follow-up questions. In fact, the danger of beginning an interview with a list of questions "written in stone" is that the list becomes a crutch that hobbles the researcher in pursuing data.

During his study of the careers of gay male prostitutes, Luckenbill (1986) consistently asked how much money his subjects made, and he was consistently given what he judged to be a grossly inflated figure. He continued asking the question, but began inconspicuously slipping in a second seemingly innocent question later in the interview: "Uh, how much money do you have on you right now?" The figure was usually only a few dollars, and he used this discrepancy to reintroduce discussion of a more accurate estimate of income. If pursued, such a seemingly simple line of inquiry begins to reveal the pathos of a life-style in which marginal members are squeezed further toward the cultural periphery of status, rewards, and opportunity, and exaggeration becomes a status-enhancing and coping strategy. The lesson here for critical ethnographers, who must be especially alert for discrepancies, is that ad-libbing subtle follow-up questions can be crucial for digging below surface appearances to search for impression-management performances that may be designed for a public audience.

Sometimes we find during data collection that our questions are not incisive, in that we are receiving answers that parrot an official party line or reflect cultural rhetoric. For example, when trying to discover how prisoners and staff may collude to bring drugs or other contraband into a prison (a crucial question for learning about how "total power" of staff is negotiated and compromised), the initial answers are likely to reflect variations on the theme that such compromises do not occur. Because of the potential vulnerability of respondents to the consequences of honest answers, the data we obtain are bland, unrevealing, and virtually worthless in illuminating the dark corners of staff-inmate interaction.

We can do one of two things: Change the topic to study data we have, or else reframe the questions. Critical ethnography may be more prone to this problem than conventional ethnography, because of the problem of digging below surface appearances. When confronted with this problem, it helps to have a few strategies for prodding. For example, when I discussed prisoner disciplinary hearings with prison staff who sat on disciplinary committees, the standard responses to questions of procedure were consistent and detailed. Unfortunately, they matched nearly word for word the official documents that specified the procedures for conducting hearings; I was asking the wrong questions in my data collection. I found the solution by first examining prior disciplinary reports, interviewing prisoners, and studying prisoner lawsuits that challenged the impropriety of hearings. I then devised questions based on the documentable policy violations. Although this strategy on occasion led to mild resistance or hostility from the interviewees, the data collected were no longer official cant but detailed explanations of the problems of prison disciplinary hearings.

As with any research, it is not a particular method that is good or bad. A data-gathering strategy is simply a tool, and as such, the appropriate questions are: (a) Is it a tool appropriate for the task? (b) Is it employed with competence? and (c) Have supplemental methodological tools been brought to bear to refine the product? The point here is that we must not look at the actual collection of data as something neutral or as something that cannot be changed. Good ethnography requires flexibility. The collection of data may be the one area where flexibility is the most crucial, because our study can be no better than the data we collect.

CONCEPTUALIZATION

Once we begin collecting our data, the project's focus should become clearer. This is not an automatic process; it occurs as we begin to appreciate more fully the cultural nuances we observe. New images spawn new questions, which in turn lead to sharper images, and at this point we can—if we have not already—begin to conceptualize more carefully the critical component of the research.

Students might begin their inquiry with a single broad interest area: What, for example, goes on in a classroom that might be of cultural interest? We may see a laid-back instructor advocating equal opportunity for all students to discuss class material, arguing for egalitarianism in class, and attempting to reduce role distance between instructor and students. Yet we observe few students participating or "acting equal." Our observations are not adequate to "explain" the discrepancy, so, still curious, we begin talking to students. We discover from casual conversations that students do not know what egalitarianism means, feel inhibited from participating for reasons that they cannot articulate, and consider the class to be one in which they "perform" as they would in every other class despite the instructor's encouragement.

From these conversations we wonder if perhaps the reasons for a nonegalitarian setting lie outside of the control of either the instructor's or the students' power. By this simple observation, we have reconceptualized a broad topic to a sharper one that now enables us to construct a few tentative questions to pursue in more formal interviews. We have moved from the study of the simple culture of a classroom to the structural factors that shape the classroom culture in ways that inhibit communication and participation.

If we pursued this study, we might find that students are not taught how to participate equally in class, and that existing hierarchical power arrangements between students and instructors create an element of distrust and role boundaries that cannot be overcome readily by interactional strategies of either group. The inertia of years of socialization to conventional schooling, the framing of appropriate classroom behavior shaped by other classes, and a preexisting structure that formats a system of evaluation and student-instructor roles and status all combine to restrict participation in an alternative classroom culture.

Now we can critically examine the social structure of a classroom as a microcosm of a form of pedagogy that is passive, that is built around power arrangements that can inhibit some teaching strategies, and that may give some students an advantage because of an ability to master roles that have little to do with learning (Aronowitz & Giroux, 1991; Bourdieu, 1991, pp. 62-63; Bourdieu & Passeron, 1979). In short, we have begun to conceptualize our topic in ways that allow for creating tentative critical working hypotheses emerging from the data.

Interpretation and Analysis

Interpretative explanation is more than creating a fancy list of typo·logical terms or labels that we impose on the data so that it "makes sense" to us. It requires attending to institutions, actions, images, utterances, events, customs, and all the usual objects of scientific interest, as well as to those on whom these objects of interest bear most heavily (Geertz, 1980, p. 167).

Interpretation of data is the *defamiliarization* process in which we revise what we have seen and translate it into something new. We bring the tentative insights we have gained back to the center of our attention "to raise havoc with our settled ways of thinking and conceptualization" (Marcus & Fischer, 1986, p. 138). Defamiliarization is a way of distancing ourselves from the taken-for-granted aspect of what we see and allowing us to view what we have seen more critically. We take the collection of observations, anecdotes, impressions, documents, and other symbolic representations of the culture we studied that seem depressingly mundane and common, and we reframe them into something new. Critical ethnography resembles literary criticism in that we look for the nonliteral meanings of our data texts. The researcher decodes the ways that the symbols of culture create asymmetrical power relations, constraining ideology, beliefs, norms, and other forces that unequally distribute social rewards, keep some people disadvantaged to the advantage of others, and block fuller participation in or understanding of our social environs. But there is something more, a value-added element. Borrowing Marx's dictum that it is not sufficient to study the world without also attempting to change it, the critical ethnographer also identifies ways by which alternative interpretations of cultural symbols can be displayed.

AN EXAMPLE: THE MAN WHO WOULD NOT DIE

My uncle died. He was in a hospital hooked up to life-support wires, tubes, and other gizmos. There were tubes for breathing, tubes for feeding, tubes to cleanse, tubes to administer drugs, and more tubes to administer drugs to counter the drugs. In a rare lucid moment, he decided to yank all support systems and go home to die with dignity, a process that was expected to occur when he slipped into a diabetic coma, which might erupt within a few hours or a day. Family, friends, clergy—all came rushing to be present in the final hours. To assure a coma would come, my uncle requested that each meal be rich, sugary, and generally as nutritionally deadly as it could be. He requested ham and eggs for his final breakfast that day. Noon came, and he, being still alive, requested pastries and snacks for his lunch, which he knew would be his final meal. He was wrong. For the last supper? Greasy pork chops.

The next morning, his wife approached the lifeless bed with an odd feeling: The bed was lifeless because it was empty. Disgruntled with others' attempts to fix the fatal meal properly, my uncle was hopping about the kitchen fixing his own. So passed the second day and another series of final meals, each as unsuccessful as the previous, and the mourners were beginning to fidget. How do you mourn a guy's death when he won't die? After nearly two weeks of "final meals," he finally departed, but so had family and friends. Dying is hard work, especially for the living, and death-managing departure rituals cannot be sustained indefinitely.

Death is more than a permanent exit. It includes what Linda Misek-Falkoff (personal communication, 1991) has called "good-bye scripts," which are prepatterned roles and lines prepared for ritual performance during exiting events. Good-bye scripts of death are formatted by class, wealth, and other factors that interweave with emotive expressions, and such scripts for dying patients can reveal much about cynicism, emotional manipulation, status, and privilege. Through interpretive analysis, the "familiar" aspects of dying become an icon for the deeper insights we glean as we pore over the data—informed by the literature that we read to sharpen our concepts—and transform it into an exciting new vision of unordinary consequence (Cullum-Swan & Manning, 1992).

When we defamiliarize our world, stairwells are no longer just avenues for moving between floors, but may be gender battlefields where women protect their space, bodies, composure, status, and identity. Classrooms are no longer a congregation of learners receiving information from a teacher, but a microcosm of discrete and overlapping manipulative struggles for status, respect, and sexual conquest, as well as ethnic hostility, degradation rituals, facework contests, and power-domination games.

Interpretation invokes and challenges the researcher's sociological imagination (Mills, 1970) by requiring continual reflection of the data and a constant search for images and metaphors that reorient individually familiar objects and frame them in a new social light. In this sense, our results are never final, but only partial and always subject to rethinking. If done well, intellectual reflections create new ways of thinking.

Discourse

Language is a form of power, because symbolizing events isolates and communicates one set of meanings and excludes others. Bourdieu (1977, pp. 170-171) contends that the power to name things is the power to organize and give meaning to experience. All linguistic exchange, and therefore all interaction, entails a form of symbolic domination in that pre-naming shapes cognition and discourse. This especially includes the "authority" of scholars, who proceed from preclassified realities while simultaneously naming and classifying new meanings (Bourdieu, 1991, pp. 72, 105-106). How we "hear" our data as they speak to us, and how we translate what we have heard into a set of messages for an audience, gives the researcher the power to define and transmit "reality." As a consequence, the discourse in which we write our results is as important as the language of the texts of the field notes that we analyze.

From our data texts come the building blocks that we use to illustrate our concepts. Sociology, as Manning (1988) reminds us, is a "language search" (p. 262) for expressing and elevating contradictions. For example, prisoners' public accounts of their relationship to correctional officers reflect a hostility ("The only good guard is a dead guard") or a set of tenets ("Never have nothing to do with a guard") that grossly contradict private behavior. The language could be interpreted as reflecting the inherent animosity that inmates express toward their keepers, and we then pass on this interpretation as if it accurately reflected the meaning of the symbols. Alternatively, we could interpret the language as a reflection of the contradictions of prison culture and the ambivalence of prisoners toward staff and recognize that language is one of the few unrestricted resources that prisoners possess.

The critical ethnographer's goal is to examine both the language of our data and the language in which we speak about our data to identify those traditions, norms, institutions, artifacts, and other characteristics of culture that provide access into the netherworld of mundane life to unblock alternative metaphors and meanings.

Reflection

Ethnographic researchers are active creators rather than passive re-corders of narratives or events. All ethnography requires systematic intellectual or personal involvement with our subjects, regardless of whether we are relying on artifacts or fully immersed with the subjects themselves. *Reflection* refers to the act of rigorously examining how this involvement affects our data gathering, analysis, and subsequent display of the data to an audience. Through reflection, an act of repeated thinking about our project, we attempt to become self-aware of the process and consequences of knowledge production by bringing the original act of knowledge back into consciousness (Gadamer, 1976, p. 45).

Sometimes we become so enmeshed in our fieldwork that we join the "other side," as did Kirkham (1976) when studying police.[2] Or we become so disillusioned with the subjects that we become cynical, patronizing, or hostile, as occurred in several students' projects on drug dealers, the homeless, and the Guardian Angels. This need not be a problem if we are aware of how the changes in perspective shape our results, so that we avoid either romanticizing or dismissing our subjects. Most changes, however, lie between the extremes of joining and casti-gating, and their effects are subtle. A few examples from my own research illustrate the problems of research changes.

While I studied prisoners for a decade, many informants became close friends of mine. In allowing me to participate in their leisure time activities and taking me through the prison as "one of them," they offered a rare, in-depth view of prison life. The consequence, however, was that I became more attuned to their problems, saw prison life from their perspective, and experienced many of the same deprivations as they did. This led me to a view of prisons from the prisoners' perspective, and although the topic of my work was prisoners, there was a danger that I might begin to romanticize the population and be excessively critical of the captors and prejudge their behavior as unnecessarily repressive in situations where it was not.

Several solutions existed to address this problem. The first would have been to maintain role distance (Adler & Adler, 1987; Goffman, 1963; Horowitz, 1983, 1986). This, while effective, removes one from a wealth of rich descriptive data and understanding. A second solution, and the path I followed, was to retain sympathy for the subjects but to write about topics that were less likely to be affected by this sympathy. This was possible by focusing on more abstract issues, such as prison discipline and jail house lawyers, that were less vulnerable to distortion by emotional attachment while still allowing prisoners to tell their story. For example, when talking to prisoners responsible for assaulting staff, the question becomes one of determining their perspective, not to justify violence, but to understand its complexity. By translating my own abhorrence of violence into a narrative containing shaded nuances of its use and abuse, the problem of appearing to glorify violence is replaced by an analysis of when and why it is employed as a normal rather than aberrant problem-solving strategy.

Above all, two primary questions should guide critical reflexivity. The first is, what is the truth quotient of the study? Here, we examine how our own values and ideology influence our work, whether we might inadvertently have excluded counterexamples that would subvert our analysis, and how our study might be different if we could redo it. The second question examines the social implications of our findings and how we present them. In this phase, we ask how our study challenges injustice and what the implications for action are. In the first question, we are demythologizing the knowledge-production process by challenging our own authority. In the second, we are asking of our study, "so what?"

Conclusion

In this chapter I have argued that critical ethnography begins as a value-laden project that directs attention to things that are not quite right in our culture. The process of actually doing critical research involves more than simply looking at culture with a jaundiced eye. It also requires that we attend to the various dimensions of topic selection, data acquisition, interpretation, and discourse to look for ways to move beyond conventional ways of observation and narrative. The goal here has not been to provide a step-by-step how-to guide, but rather to indicate that the act of critical ethnography is made up of many discrete components, each of which offer potential for refining our final product.

NOTES

1. Lukacs (1971b, pp. 93-94) distinguishes between critical realism and socialist realism. The primary difference between the two is that critical realism fails to develop a socialist agenda.

2. A thin line divides "going native" with "going over to the other side." *Going native* means that we become immersed so fully in our fieldwork or with our subjects that we become acculturated, and our identity is enmeshed with the culture we study. This poses the risk of loss of objectivity, but it is not necessarily undesirable as long as we remember that we are scientists. Some researchers select topics that are a part of their culture, such as student life, Alcoholics Anonymous, or subway riding. *Going over to the other side,* however, means that we give up our scientific persona and substitute the norms of the new culture for the canons of science. Going native in some cases may be acceptable; going over to the other side is not.

4. EMPIRICAL APPLICATION

In this chapter, I will move from general principles of implementing a critical approach to concrete examples. Three interrelated examples drawn from my own research on prisoner litigation, prison violence, and computer hacking illustrate how ethnography can raise critical themes. Although there are many examples of critical ethnography, I use mine because I am responsible for and can therefore speak to and defend the intent of my own words. Each project began with a large subgroup or interest. Smaller questions moved center stage during data collection as the clash between the self-perceptions of the subcultures and the meanings imputed to them by the dominant culture came into focus.

Prisoner Litigation and
Existential Rebellion

Maximum security prisons are dreadful places and those in them are usually prone to violence.[1] Prison culture is often considered the product of one of two sources: Prisoners bring nasty habits into the institution with them, and expressing these habits creates a rather unpleasant environment (importation model), or prison deprivations impel prisoners to respond and cope in a manner that creates a debilitating culture (deprivation model). These are neither mutually exclusive nor exhaustive possibilities, but variants dominate the literature of prison culture (Bowker, 1977; DiIulio, 1987, pp. 13-17). The consequence is that our understanding of prisons focuses on prisoner or institutional pathology, rather than on the meanings that the cultural acts possess for the participants. One example of viewing prisoner behavior as a reflection of antisocial tendencies occurs in attempts to understand prisoner litigation, and an existential model is offered as an alternative.

Prisoner litigation refers to inmate suits, usually filed by inmates skilled in legal matters ("jail house lawyers," or JHLs) in federal court to challenge conviction proceedings or prison conditions and policies. Critics of prisoner litigation tend to explain it by alluding to prisoners' disruptive behavior on the streets becoming translated into disruptive litigation in prison, as nothing more than "bored inmates with time on their hands" who enjoy hassling their keepers, or as unfair attempts by convicted felons to seek release after fair conviction proceedings (D. Anderson, 1986; Reed, 1980). These explanations reduce the meanings of JHLs' behavior to a reflection of some undesirable characteristic and divert attention from the motives for litigation by attacking the credibility of those engaged in it. By recasting the meaning of prisoner litigation, we gain a better understanding of its sources and purposes as well as a broader picture of prison existence. Two simple questions emerged from my research: (a) How do prisoners account for their litigation and over what do they litigate, and (b) what themes unify these accounts? The concept of *existential rebellion,* creating meaning through resistance, is one integrating answer.

SUMMARY OF THE DATA

The study of jail house lawyers did not begin with the intent of analyzing their culture. It began instead as a general question: What problems do prisoners encounter in college courses that differ from students on a college campus? In examining the obstacles to prison education, it became clear that it was first necessary to understand the prison culture. JHLs, as one significant component in responding to its problems, emerged as one of many possible icons for prison culture, because their experiences embodied its best and worst characteristics.

I interviewed jail house lawyers, federal judges, and others to examine the litigation process and reasons why prisoners sued (Thomas, 1988, pp. 17-22). The common thread that unified JHL activity was clearly the metaphor of resistance. The reasons for resistance provided insights into how law became a tool for "saying no" and for challenging what, to prisoners, was an unacceptable situation.

Prison culture is complex, and the competing rules, value systems, and power sources make it seem mysterious, capricious, and over-whelming to prisoners. Litigation clearly served a number of purposes, all of which reflected a response to these conditions. Litigation was a form of self-help that some inmates used to better themselves and their environment. It was used to negotiate problems in situations where violence might otherwise have been used, and it provided a safety valve for easing some of the potentially volatile situations that can arise in prison culture. Litigation provided a way to challenge abuse of power by some staff, to rectify staff indifference when confronted with prisoners' bureaucratic problems (e.g., release date), and to subvert the hierarchy of informal power by using law to enforce "rule following" by staff. But it also entailed risks, such as loss of a case or retaliation by prison staff or other inmates.

ORGANIZING THEME:
AN EXISTENTIAL VIEW OF LITIGATION

An *organizing theme* or concept is a single category by which loose threads of data can be unified into a clearly imaged tapestry. For all ethnographers, one helpful analytic strategy involves using analogous concepts or metaphors drawn from other disciplines to translate seem-ingly alien meanings into something more familiar. An existential perspective borrowed from literature (Friedman, 1973; Goodwin, 1971) provided a way to "make sense" of the data. A central theme of existen-tialism is that when the conditions of life seem to preclude meaningful and effective action, people find meaning in resistance and in the act of saying no. Existentialism depicts the individual as faced with the dilemma of choosing between acquiescence and resistance, on the one hand, and constraints and freedom on the other (Camus, 1956; Sartre, 1955).

Prison life becomes an analogue for other forms of social existence in which the potential to act is obstructed and social actors remain powerless relative to their potential to engage and transcend their cir-cumstances. Choices are suppressed, organizational identities are im-posed, and one becomes what the environment dictates. For JHLs, law empowers those convicted of violating it with a weapon for challenging their environment.

Although one cannot necessarily impute to JHLs themselves an existential consciousness, their acts, in the aggregate, range from individual resistance to sophisticated political action. Their litigation reflects a form of resistance to unnecessary and oppressive forms of social control that leads us to label them "primitive rebels." Reminiscent of the characters in the works of Sartre (1947) or Camus (1955, 1958), existential protagonists, though not particularly noteworthy, attain a certain nobility, even heroism, through acts of resistance.

WHY IS THIS CRITICAL?

The primary critical consequence of this project lies in the reconceptualization of jail house law. The findings challenged those who used the metaphor of pathology to curtail prisoners' civil rights. Contrary to critics' claims, there was no evidence that prisoners' litigious activity was pathological or meaningless. Like Sisyphus, who suffered for his rebellious acts against the gods (Camus, 1955), jail house lawyering reflects the existential freedom that allows one to influence the future and to participate in molding social existence through acts of resistance that may provoke retaliation. The findings require a reexamination of prisoner litigation and the role of law as a means of prison reform, rather than dismissing it as a waste of judicial time and taxpayers' money (Brakel, 1987).

A secondary critical consequence of the study lies in the broader question of how institutional and other social arrangements place people at a power disadvantage, confront them with double binds, and constrain behavior and consciousness. From a relatively simple study of jail house lawyers, it raises questions about how people recognize and mediate an oppressive culture, even if in ironic and often futile ways.

The Violence of Racial Meanings in Prison Culture

The previous example reconceptualized the meaning of the behavior of a specific group (jail house lawyers). This section shifts from the meaning of a label to the broader social consequences that flow from symbolic identities. For example, one's racial identity is a sign system that sends off cues that allocate power and privilege; establish social,

52

political, and other boundaries; shape interaction; provide a signifying context for action; and serve as an account-generating mechanism to explain behavior.[2] Race in prisons illustrates this process.

Racism in prisons occurs not only because of discriminatory practices, but also because one's race connotes and denotes sets of meanings that define how one "does time." The label *nigger* is more than just a hostile epithet. It also carries connotative conceptual baggage and implications for social interpretation and policy. Race becomes a metaphor that conveys pictures about how prisoners should act in dealing with the "niggers" to whom the images pertain. Racially imbued images take on the character of social myths by creating accounts, normative judgments, and actions directed toward a subordinate culture. The myths reproduce power relations by creating and consolidating icons that reinforce stigma, define societal responses, and establish the boundaries between the sacred dominant groups and profane subordinate ones.

SUMMARY OF THE DATA

Like many topics, this subject was not so much "chosen" as it was an emergent theme from one slice of a massive body of prisoner narratives. The significance of racial identity grew out of my experience as, with only rare exceptions, the only Caucasian in prison interactions. I realized how my own identity often restricted my understandings of normal conversations. My ignorance of the common stock of shared knowledge on which interaction was built led to an understanding that "whiteness" was both a powerful resource (when employed to maintain social status) and a liability (when its social meaning was attacked).

Whites. We generally are blinded to the fact that the meaning of the racial experience is not the same for whites and nonwhites. Because of many complex nuances, race is a resource that can be used by whites and a stigma to be managed by nonwhites. The cues embedded in race and ethnicity shape the prison experience for whites by providing an identity, behavioral codes, and effective responses that include suspicion, fear, or hostility. Whites, especially those with little previous association with other ethnic cultures, may interpret another's race as a cue that symbolizes the terror of prisons, because whites in maximum security prisons are likely to be in the minority.

For whites, racial identity promotes white unity by conferring a set of hostile meanings upon nonwhites. These meanings provide a code that devalues the stigmatized group through hostile discourse that separates "decent" criminals from presumably indecent ones. The comments of one white Illinois prisoner provide an illustration:

> Generally, blacks create the biggest problem. As a group they are uneducated, and they have no respect for the rights of others. They are the predators for the most part, and they are cowards. The only way they exist is by the gang. Alone, all they have is a big mouth, and no common sense. In many cases the Puerto Ricans are worse than the blacks. They are noisemakers from morning to night. The ideal solution would be for all the Latinos in this country to swim south with a nigger under each arm . . . then shoot them like sharks.

The hostility expressed in such views polarizes prisoners by creating a series of damaging metaphors (e.g., as animalistic, as social misfits, and as targets of violence) and by providing a rhetorical strategy that justifies continued animosity and mortification rituals (Goffman, 1961, p. 14). These metaphors translate symbols into "literals" that provide myths about both prison life and other prisoners that may influence how new white inmates respond to their initial immersion in the culture.

Staff racial favoritism benefits whites in job assignments and other rewards, as well as in discretionary application of institutional policies. Some white inmates manipulate racial stereotypes to obtain preferential treatment, as occurred when a white prisoner intended to have some nonwhites assault him to emphasize his vulnerability and thus assure his transfer to another institution. A white gay prisoner used staff animosity against blacks to secure a transfer when he wrote a document detailing gang activities and gave it to officials. It was claimed that he then leaked the information that he had done this to fellow prisoners to assure that he would be "marked for a hit" (a planned inmate assault), which assured the transfer. Another white inmate explained how he invoked the threat of potential racial violence to obtain a transfer to a trustee position in the event of a guilty verdict for several prisoners being tried for murdering prison guards at Pontiac.

The ability of whites to use the race game intentionally typifies one subtle advantage they possess that nonwhites do not: The images of nonwhites as violent and predatory create a resource for manipulating staff. This manipulation in turn exploits and reinforces these images. Racial meanings become a polarizing resource that makes doing time a bit easier for whites at the expense of nonwhites.

Non-Whites. Even when nonwhite prisoners may be in the majority, racial abuse permeates their prison experience in dramatic and subtle ways. For example, one black activist inmate complained that he left his locked cell and returned to find that someone with access to keys (presumably one or more guards) had entered and painted racial epithets and Ku Klux Klan messages on the walls. He interpreted this as a message intended to intimidate him into compliance with institutional white norms. The message, he said, was clear: "White was right," and staff would be among those to remind him. Nonwhites arriving at an institution confront a white power structure more directly than those on the streets. For many, it is the first time they have ever had sustained interaction with whites. Despite occasional interracial friendships, there remains an ambience of suspicion, mistrust, and in some institutions, open warfare.

Nonwhites accommodate to prison culture by joining gangs. Gangs compete for resources along racial lines and create a quasi-independent subculture within the culture with its own social organization, values, economic system, and social control mechanisms. These continuing racial divisions block recognition of shared problems by prisoners, and they perpetuate the tension between a white administrative power structure and a nonwhite prisoner social order.

ORGANIZING THEME: SYMBOLIC VIOLENCE

The data reveal that the sign system embedded in racial identity is violent. Racial identity imposes metaphors that wrench prisoners out of their shared humanity and creates conditions that exacerbate qualities such as animosity, distrust, and predation. Racial images are violent because they arbitrarily impose symbols in ways that may grotesquely distort the reality of what is seen and what is signified by what is seen. The distortions reflect oppressive power relations that promote the interests of the more powerful. Culturally imposed meanings are political, and the political meanings of these categories provide a coded text (i.e., an integrated set of symbols that provide the rules and vocabulary for deciphering the significance of race) that forcefully shapes cultural power and privilege.

The concept of prison violence evokes images of inmates assaulting others. It rarely includes symbolic violence. Racial codes are violent because they create images that correspond to ideologies of suppression by whites and oppression of blacks. These ideological simulacra (images taken as the "thing itself") become the reality and form the icons that guide behavior. They disrupt the social fabric by creating racially embedded symbols that can be manipulated at the expense of one group for the advantage of another.

Racial codes are also violent because they create structural barriers that preclude some groups from access to resources available to others. Exclusionary systems of resource allocation influenced by racial factors add punitive sanctions to prison life. Individual meanings, norms, expectations, and behavioral strategies (e.g., violence or withdrawal) combine to form the structural elements of rules, power, and organization.

WHY IS THIS CRITICAL?

Racism is more than bigotry, prejudice, or discriminatory behavior. *Institutionalized racism* sustains structural barriers functioning to distribute social rewards. Racism is the aggregate set of social factors that give one group power at the expense of another, and part of this asymmetrical power process includes the symbols denoting and connoting racial meanings. Racism is an ideology in that it furnishes the shared conceptual symbols for organizing interracial experience. These symbols contribute to turmoil in prisons by shaping an inescapable aspect of existence that is debilitating for all inmates and staff and subverts administrative efforts to deliver parity in resources and to assure a safe existence. Shifting the focus in prisons away from the conceptual dichotomy of interaction (or structure of white versus black) to race as a communicative system of significations allows its complexity to be recognized more fully.

In Defense of the Computer Underground

The growth of computer technology has created a new type of social demon as the "techno-revolution" challenges definitions of law, property rights, privacy, and conventional social control strategies.[3] This has led to law enforcement fears that some subcultures may possess or utilize the means to acquire, manipulate, or transmit knowledge in potentially predatory ways. One consequence of this has been the application

56

of concepts of "crime" or "deviance" to new behaviors perceived to have analogues to old ones. The result, in the case of "computer abuse," is the criminalization of seemingly socially threatening behavior. The computer underground (CU) illustrates this.

THE CULTURE OF THE COMPUTER UNDERGROUND

The CU is a broad and somewhat overlapping invisible community comprising people who systematically interact electronically on computer bulletin board systems (BBSs) by means of personal computers and telephone modems in order to engage in a variety of shared activities. A BBS, the focal point of CU activity, is a computer equipped with software that others call and communicate with each other through by leaving messages and exchanging computer programs or text files. CU activities vary and include *hacking* (computer intrusion), *phreaking* (free long-distance telephone dialing), and *piracy* (sharing copyrighted computer software).

In response to this new form of "deviance," law enforcement has aggressively stigmatized and attacked those they perceive as a subversive threat to the control of information and technology. This has led to crackdowns on "deviants," to anti-computer underground media campaigns, and to hasty revision of state and federal statutes (Sterling, 1992).

SUMMARY OF THE DATA

Like many topics, the choice of the computer underground as a research project was serendipitous. It began as the result of a student thesis into which I was drawn; I found the media depictions conflicting with the student's findings. This led to my own inquiry into the dissonance between participants' meanings and broader cultural meanings. The gap between what the legal system was believed to enforce and what it actually enforced provided the analytic focal point.

The data revealed that considerable legislation, fueled by media and law enforcement hyperbole that dramatized the dangers of "computer crime" (Hollinger & Lanza-Kaduce, 1988), created an image for simple behaviors ranging from computer intrusion and software piracy that resembled such serious felonies as computer theft, espionage, theft of trade secrets, and residential burglary (Conly, 1989; McEwen, 1989).

This led to enactment of laws and application of recent federal seizure policies that, in effect, targeted computer abusers with the same fury as drug and other serious crimes. Our data, however, revealed a culture quite different from that portrayed in the media and legislative debates. Among other findings, we discovered that the computer underground reflects a highly complex mosaic of interests, motives, and skills and possesses a language and a set of values, information-processing techniques, and norms that shape its cultural identity. Most CU participants are law-abiding. Even on so-called elite BBSs, illicit activity is more frequently discussed than practiced. The data suggest that in the main, the vast majority of CU participants stridently oppose "trashing" (disrupting other computer systems), "carding" (obtaining free long-distance calls by using stolen credit card numbers), and all forms of related malicious or illegal behavior.

Whatever their individual motives or intents, the CU can be understood as a form of social rebellion in some ways analogous to the counterculture of the 1960s. It is not necessarily an intentional attempt to resist social norms, but it reflects nonetheless a socially situated tension with political and ideological overtones. It is political to the extent that it challenges existing forms of power and control, and ideological because it challenges beliefs and policies about computer system security, information as private property, and other established social and legal premises.

Law enforcement investigations of hacker activity entail methods considered unacceptable in other forms of criminal investigation (Kapor, 1991; Schwartz, 1990; Sterling, in press). These include excessively broad search warrants, confiscation of property unrelated to suspected offenses, and privacy invasions that include warrantless surveillance.[4] Crackdowns on the CU during the past few years appear to be more symbolic than substantively effective. Ironically, crackdowns may even contribute to the very behaviors they seek to control. Several findings lead to this conclusion: (a) Licit or only marginally illicit users are dropping out, thus decreasing the socializing processes that formerly discouraged serious predations; (b) the secrecy and inaccessibility of the culture to outsiders, which in the past was more symbolic than real, is now becoming a necessity for those committed to continuing illegal behavior; and (c) as the consequences for violating the law increase, the stakes for which the law is violated also may increase.

ORGANIZING THEME: REPRESSIVE LAW

The data reveal two conflicting factors. The first is the emergence of a counterculture of computer-literate persons able to challenge the control of information technology by circumventing established laws and societal norms when using technology as a plaything. The second is the resistance of a dominant social order to this new culture. Through the stigmatization process, the symbols of CU culture (e.g., "hacker handles" or aliases, vocabulary, participation on hacker BBSs) become the crime itself, and a control backlash has led to public suspicion, law enforcement sweeps that produce much media attention but few indictments, and a series of broad laws attempting with little success to reduce "computer crime."

The data suggested several tentative conclusions to help understand the discrepancy between the laws and what the laws were intended to control. We live in an era of state intervention and social engineering, one characteristic of which is the legislation against a variety of "profane" behaviors that violate an accepted moral order and invoke the criminal justice process.

In addition, new technology has increased faster than social understanding, laws, legislative statutes, or enforcement strategies can match. Prior to the computer revolution, the definition of information and the regulation of the technology that created and the media that conveyed it evolved over several centuries of statute and case law. Violations generally were considered a matter for civil rather than criminal law. The increased emphasis on information as a commodity and on the enforcement of property claims associated with commodity protection has shifted the norms and ideology away from accessibility toward proprietary exclusivity. The result has been an increase in federal and state criminal statutes protecting both computer systems and their products (Hollinger & Lanza-Kaduce, 1988) and a growing awareness that criminal prosecution is a strong option for computer trespassing (Conly, 1989; McEwen, 1989).

The invocation of the criminal justice system against specific groups or behaviors follows a "moral panic" in which the targeted groups undergo a ritualized symbolic transformation. They become defined not as inquiring amateurs or benign nuisances, but as profaners of the sacred moral order (Cohen, 1980). This transformation is a form of *scapegoating,* in which public troubles are traced to and blamed on the scapegoats.

Although sometimes the scapegoats are guilty of some antisocial act, the response exceeds the harm of the act, and the targets are pursued not only for what they may have done, but also for the stigmatizing signs they bear (Girard, 1985). This transformative process and the corresponding enforcement of the behaviors that emerge from it resemble what, in earlier times, were called witch hunts. Agents of control, responding to the panic, actively seek out those whose social identity has been transformed in a systematic and highly visible manner (Bergeson, 1977; Currie, 1968; Erikson, 1966).

We can also see a postmodernist political subtext layered beneath hacker activity that reflects a gap between technology and its social understanding. Like jail house lawyers, computer underground participants create meaning through dissonance. Participation stems from a quest for knowledge, a sense of rebelliousness, and the enjoyment of risk taking. The risks entailed by acting on the fringes of legality, substituting social definitions of acceptable behavior with their own, the playful parodying of mass culture, and the challenge to authority constitute an exploration of the limits of culture while resisting the legal meanings that would control such actions. The celebration of antiheroes, reenacted through forays into the world of computer programs and software, reflects the stylistic promiscuity, eclecticism, and blurring of the boundaries of reality that typifies the postmodern experience. Instead of embracing the dominant culture, the CU has created an irreducible cultural alternative, one that cannot be understood without locating its place within the dialectic of social change.

WHY IS THIS CRITICAL?

The data indicate that the gap between law and its enforcement has led to serious challenges by police officials and prosecutors to constitutional rights that include freedom of speech and privacy both in what constitutes protected electronic "speech" and in how investigations of computer crime proceed. By examining the creative hyperbole used by law enforcement to justify raids and the creative prosecution employed to target hackers, we are given insights into the process by which a new form of "deviance" emerges, is defined as dangerous, and is targeted for control.

The criminalization of "deviant" acts transforms and reduces societal meanings to legal ones, but legal meanings often distort alternative interpretations. The Manichean imagery conveyed by legal definitions tends to direct attention away from the social significance of deviant acts by portraying them as an evil to be eradicated. This study of the computer underground is critical because it uses information from a small subculture as a way to understand and challenge the inappropriate use of law in targeting "deviants" whose primary threat is simply that they are different.

Conclusion

Each of these examples typifies the ways in which critical analysis can be applied to fairly mundane topics by moving beyond the immediate narrative of the subjects to the broader processes in which the narratives are embedded. Jail house lawyers create dissonance and change their environment, racial meanings generate a resource that provides some with a tool for gaining power at the expense of those who lack the same resource, and computer underground participants generate a counterculture that challenges conventional legal and social norms and values. In each of the examples above, the ultimate topic emerged by identifying an organizational theme or concept that seemed to penetrate most deeply into social processes of cultural control.

The broader social implications of these studies varied. The analyses of prisoner litigation and race in prisons carried no overt call for action. Each, however, posed a challenge. The former empirically demonstrated that many of the premises of those attempting to curtail prisoners' rights are inaccurate. The latter illustrated the destructive nature of symbolic violence in prisons. Both studies reflected attempts to change ways of thinking and to provide evidence to counter accepted views. The study of computer hackers was a wider call for action. In addition to questioning dominant perceptions, it supplemented others' efforts in legislative and policy reform by using the data to illustrate an erosion of constitutional protections. The study was also the basis of the formation of an electronic newsletter, *Computer underground Digest (CuD)*, distributed to more than 40,000 readers across computer networks to share information about legal and political concerns.

It is by developing an appreciation of difference and showing how these differences may mirror social problems, power, control, irony, and suppression in the dominant culture that we begin to do critical ethnography and on occasion find ways to apply the knowledge directly to action.

NOTES

1. The data and discussion for this section are drawn from Thomas (1988) and Milovanovic and Thomas (1989).
2. The data for this discussion come from Thomas (1992).
3. The following data and discussion come from Meyer and Thomas (1990) and Thomas and Meyer (1990, 1991).
4. For detailed discussions of constitutional rights and electronic communication, see especially the electronic journals available on Internet devoted to these issues, including EFFector Online at eff@eff.org and *Computer underground Digest* at tk0jut2@mvs.cso.niu.edu. Detailed legal summaries are available through internet/anonymous ftp at ftp.eff.org.

5. CONCLUSION: TRICKS, TRAPS, AND MOVING BEYOND

Two difficult questions confront critical scholars. The first centers on how we remain scientific while simultaneously practicing critique. The second asks why we should bother to be critical at all. The answer to the first is one of technique, and there are a few broad guidelines that help keep us on track. The second answer is primarily a personal one, and I offer my own justification for engaging in critical research.

Critical ethnography begins from the premise that knowledge is a resource as powerful as any tangible tool. As a tool, new ways of thinking become implements by which we can *act upon* our world instead of passively being *acted upon*. Joll (1978, p. 119) reminds us that we can affect our own personal development and that of our surroundings only when we have a reasonably clear view of the nature of our culture and what possibilities for action are open to us. Critical ethnography attempts to provide clearer images of the larger picture of which we are a part. Once the picture takes on sharper detail, opportunities for revising it take shape.

Critical thinking does not stop when a single research project ends, because it is a way of life. The insights and knowledge gained from research extend into other realms beyond simply professional interest. They draw attention to how preexisting cultural formations shape behavioral opportunities and life chances; how cultural participants reaffirm, challenge, or accommodate to existing cultural formations; and how culture is re-created continually with every word, gesture, and act.

Critical thinking simply means taking the sociological imagination seriously by shifting from discrete instances of phenomena to their broader social context. Knowledge production is not easy, however, and perils lurk that threaten to subvert our studies by confining them to the realm of polemics.

Traps and Tricks

Before embarking on individual projects, novice critical thinkers should remember that there are several traps awaiting them. Falling into the traps often dooms a study to simply another polemical exercise that is passionately rhetorical but scientifically unpersuasive. The traps are most likely to occur in the interpretation and writing phase as our passion for the topic threatens to conquer our scientific persona, but several tricks help to avoid these problems.

Trap 1: Seeing only what serves our purposes
Trick 1: Avoid imposing meanings on data

The data should "speak" to us, and we should listen closely, even if what we hear is not to our liking. To do otherwise is not only bad science, it is intellectually dishonest and unethical. If the data contradict or demonstrate processes counter to our expectations, we must then change our position to fit the data. I learned this lesson early when writing my dissertation. I intended to demonstrate that federal funding of policing studies was repressive and systematically excluded critical research that "threatened capitalism." The naïveté of this proposition aside, the data provided no evidence that funding agencies repressed critical (or "leftist") research, and in fact suggested that agencies encouraged it. The problem appeared to be the lack of critically inclined funding applicants (Thomas, 1980). Although an embarrassing lesson, it nonetheless reinforced the adage that one must never anticipate what will be found in a way that creates a built-in antagonism prior to data gathering.

Trap 2: Using conceptual clichés
Trick 2: Avoid buzzwords

The temptation to fall into a "jargon trap" (Van Maanen, 1988, p. 28) when writing up results can lead to exaggerated claims and distorted conclusions. There is no need to talk about "oppressive fascist racists," or to try to import into our discussion concepts such as "class struggle," "state oppression," or similar terms that we might use more informally in casual conversation, but that have no direct bearing on our study. If a specific term, such as *class,* is explicitly relevant to our analysis and discussion, it is legitimate to use. Gottdeiner (1982) and Williams (1985) successfully demonstrate this in their respective analyses of Disneyland and "capitalist social formation" and gentrification, class, and community conflict. Nonetheless, employing broad categories for dramatic rhetorical effect rather than as conceptually tight organizing themes risks weakening analysis and diluting the utility of the terms. All ethnography should demonstrate, not assert, and the best critical ethnographies simply describe the terrain and let the readers evaluate the conclusions on the basis of what has been shown.

Effective critique need never be packaged as critical. Rather, it should lead the reader, step by step, through the data with as little prompting as possible by painting a picture in sufficiently sharp detail that readers will be convinced by the power of the demonstration, rather than by the passion of the researcher. One good example is Manning's (1977) *Police Work*, which on its surface is a dramaturgical analysis of how police do their job. In reality, it is a devastating portrayal of the impossibility of the police crime-fighting mandate. In showing how the symbols of crime fighting replace the reality of it, Manning avoids all use of catch-phrases and simply lays out the data in a way that leads the reader to the conclusion that police work involves creating the illusion of fighting crime as much as actually protecting the commonweal.

Trap 3: Placing passion before science
Trick 3: Avoid ax grinding

The goal of critical ethnography is to bring data to bear on a topic, not to attack a favorite target. Most people recognize that there are social problems, and a study need not begin by castigating a particular group as unjust or oppressive. This means that the concluding section of a paper should be tight, remain true to the data, and not move beyond in a wild orgy of verbal bloodletting in which the researcher moves from interpretation of insights to yelling "revolution" from the rooftop in the dark. Good ethnography allows the reader to draw conclusions from the data, because unless the materials speak to both the issues and the audience clearly, they are of no substantive value.

Few people consciously support bigotry or the cultural features that promote it. As a consequence, self-righteous indignation is not only ineffective, but diverts attention away from empirically based conclusions by masking them beneath unnecessary preaching. The adage "KISMIF"—keep it simple, make it fun—is as true for writing up results as it is for summer camp: Anger at injustice should not be channeled into polemics, but into accurate data and straightforward presentation with as little extraneous editorializing as possible.

Trap 4: Making claims beyond demonstrable evidence
Trick 4: Avoid overgeneralizing

Glaser and Strauss (1967, pp. 37, 52, 242-244) remind us that the generalizability of all qualitative research should be treated with caution. Care must be taken not to assume that what we find in one population holds true for all other populations or situations, and the credibility of our study diminishes when we leap from particularistic claims drawn from our study to universal assertions.

When examining "repressive behavior," it is unwise to attribute malice when stupidity or conformity to group standards suffices. This simply means that it is bad form to attribute political motives to individuals or groups when we are looking instead at interactional processes that operate independently from explicit political intentions. Likewise, we must never combine claims we wish to be taken as accurate with those claims we intend to be suggestive. For example, the fact that men enjoy greater social advantages than women does not mean that "men create a society so they can oppress women." Cultural formations evolve slowly and often imperceptibly, and beneficiaries of advantage may be unaware not only of the social formations that contribute to their position, but even that they benefit at others' expense. We can demonstrate that women are (or are not) disadvantaged in relation to men in a given area, but to assume that this demonstrates concerted intentional action by males is an overgeneralization for which data, if they exist, must be presented. Overgeneralizing means that we speak beyond the data, and the analysis should not exceed what the data show. It is fully appropriate, however, to place in a separate concluding section a cautious conjecture about broader issues and directions for subsequent research.

Trap 5: Replacing reason with stridency
Trick 5: Avoid sledgehammers

Subtlety is nearly always preferable to repeatedly hitting the reader over the head with data-free assertions, especially when those assertions challenge comfortable images and ideas. It cannot be repeated enough: Good ethnography illustrates rather than asserts, and if a point cannot be demonstrated empirically, then it should not be asserted. The "sledgehammer" syndrome is most common in studies that lack (or are unconcerned with) data and therefore must rely on simplified rhetoric, as did much radical criminology of early 1970s. The cogency of an argument lies in the data. One can creatively explore issues in a concluding section on implications or directions for further research, but a clear distinction must be made between conclusions that are empirically based and the more freewheeling discussion of conjecture and next-step suggestions. Empirical analysis should be thought of as a scalpel, not a cudgel, and the metaphor of incisiveness is more effective than the metaphor of battering.

Trap 6: Writing to the already committed
Trick 6: Remember the audience

The adage "take the revolution to where it ain't" should guide how we address the audience: We should not be preaching to those already convinced of our ideas, but instead attempting to reach those who are not. Preaching to the choir may garner a few accolades from those who agree with us, but if the goal is one of convincing others of the credibility of our claims, we must always ask who those "others" are. The discourse of our final paper differs depending on whether we are writing a paper for a class, an article for a highly specialized journal, or a letter to the editor. Students may feel disadvantaged by the added agenda of the instructor's power of the grade. This may lead to a manipulative presentational strategy based on what it appears the instructor wants written, rather than on what the canons of science suggest ought to be written. The best strategy lies in anticipating the strongest argument that critics of both our science and our perspective might raise, then analyzing and speaking accordingly. A canon for all science is that intellectual integrity is never sacrificed to expediency.

There is nothing wrong with writing to an audience of one, because sometimes it is effective to select a specific person as a representative of a larger population. It helps to identify an intellectual opponent and ask, how must I write to present convincing evidence? A good rule of thumb is to remember that all ethnography is a dual translation process. We are translating the cultural codes of our subjects into a symbolic form that we can understand. We then translate our understandings into a form that the audience can understand. We must therefore be fluent in three languages: that of the subjects, that of our own science, and that of the audience.

Sometimes we may feel that we are watering down the content of our ideas in the translation process, but if the audience either will not understand it or, if it understands, will dismiss it, then we have failed to translate properly. All research is a communication enterprise, and our guiding principle should be one of finding ways to communicate what we feel is important in a language understandable to our audience.

Trap 7: Forgetting the ethnographic project
Trick 7: Appreciate difference

To provide the audience with an appreciation of difference and with an increased understanding of the culture we study is not the same as romanticizing our subjects. In analyzing stigmatized populations, the goal is not only to convey a common humanity, but more important, to show similarities between these and conventional populations by juxtaposing the unfamiliar with more familiar concepts. For example, a student studying "racists" retained her hostility toward them but developed a greater appreciation for their fears, feelings, and the role that race played in establishing group solidarity. Her goal was not to justify or condone, but to understand in ways that would allow her to confront the problem more effectively in social interaction and student government. To appreciate difference means to disrupt common sense and place unfamiliar objects in a new context. When this is done successfully, we are rewarded with insights into the culture of study that prompt us to think about our own culture in new ways by searching for analogous concepts that make the alien culture seem more familiar and our own culture seem more alien.

Critical ethnography is *emancipatory*, and our analytic discourse aims to unshackle comfortable ways of viewing the world. We do this by remembering the story is that of our subjects, and we translate their narrative into a conceptual and theoretical story of our own. Because the language we use creates the images we convey, the researcher should be conscious of the best stylistic device appropriate for translating what seems important to an audience. Writing is communication, and a literary style that includes pathos (sorrow), bathos (biting hyperbole), or even parody (playfulness) is generally more effective than a stream-of-consciousness presentation of data (Antonio, 1991; Burke, 1989; Richardson, 1991; Van Maanen, 1988).

Trap 8: Taking ourselves as given
Trick 8: Discover reflexively who we are

Ethnography is as much talk about the data as it is analysis of the data, and attention to how we talk about data requires that we reflect on who we are and what we say (Agar, 1986; Geertz, 1988; Van Maanen, 1988). We turn away from the belief that we have spoken truly and turn instead to the question, how have we spoken? The researcher is part and parcel of the research process, and we must always be aware not only of how we might influence and shape the slice of culture we study, but must also of how we ourselves are changed by the research process. Reflexive understanding is a form of self-dialogue by which we demythologize (i.e., strip away comfortable meanings from) what we have done. Although many of the questions we ask can be abstract and philosophical (e.g., "What are the epistemological foundations of my study?"), most are relatively simple. Examples of the latter include, "How would my study be done differently if done with statistical analysis?", "What are the ethical implications of the research?", and "How did the research change me or my subjects?"

When our views change, the focus of our study changes, because new views open up new horizons from which to draw questions and tentative answers. When our focus changes, we begin to ask different questions, reorganize data to correspond to the new ideas, and redefine the nature of the original problem. It is also possible, as occurred in my computer underground research, that probing for some types of information will create a new awareness by the participants. This, in turn, changes their narratives, their behaviors, and their own "onstage performances" in ways that alter the topic. In some of my own discussions with hackers and pirates, the interaction provoked some subjects to rethink illicit behavior in ways that ultimately shaped their talk by altering either their behaviors or their accounts of it. This is neither good nor bad, but if it does occur, the researcher must be not only alert but prepared to include the changes as part of the analysis.

Many of the pitfalls threatening critical scholars inhere in all research, but they are more obvious when the researcher announces, rather than hides, the intention to engage in a visibly value-laden project. The trick to doing "objective" critical ethnography lies in avoiding the traps of creating a product of assertions rather than demonstrable claims and of imposing our own views both on the data and on the audience. Attending to these problems requires more patience, thought, and skill than required in conventional research, and it is inherently more messy. When done well, however, the final product can be exciting and rewarding, because we are no longer the same person as when we started.

Why Be Critical?

A researcher's perspective is largely a matter of personal predilection, and one obviously is free to choose whatever intellectual orientation is most comfortable. Why, then, should one adopt a critical stance when it is both more difficult and riskier than conventional research? The answer is partly normative and partly practical. There are many reasons to prefer critical to conventional thought, and they can be collapsed into several broad categories: personal satisfaction, intellectual responsibility, emancipatory potential, and ethical obligation.

Some researchers on all sides of the political spectrum are interested in social issues, and a critical perspective provides a satisfying way to integrate the private and professional spheres of existence. Bringing data to bear on social issues, whether for the purpose of affecting policy or of expanding knowledge and understanding, is one way of adapting our scientific expertise to the world around us.

There are also intrinsic rewards that derive from critical thinking. The excitement of reworking concepts and creating new ways of seeing culture provides some scholars with sufficient justification to pursue this perspective despite the barriers to acceptance of their ideas. Fighting against social inertia—the tendency for people to resist the discomfort of challenges to their sacred images of everyday life—is, for some, an exhilarating challenge. Reworking cultural myths and deflating accepted notions of cultural order that attain dominance without any demonstrable intellectual justification may seem like jousting with the occasional windmill. But for persons who enjoy challenging sacred cultural icons, critical thought becomes a resource, and the results can be measured by the degree to which our data and analysis convey to others something that they did not previously recognize.

Intellectual obligation provides a second justification for critical involvement. Intellectuals, as Karl Mannheim (1938) observed, tend to transform conflicts of interest into theoretical challenges, making the development of knowledge socially contingent. The goal of science ought to be more than uncovering the superficial characteristics of the presumed objective characteristics of a world "out there" (Lynd, 1939/1970). The validity of making claims ultimately lies in the investigation of an object, but investigation occurs in a social context in which prepatterned assumptions shape the ordering of the investigative experience (Mannheim, 1938, p. 4). Without recognizing the socially contingent nature of knowledge and the researcher's background and domain assumptions (Gouldner, 1970, pp. 29-37) that shape social inquiry, partial knowledge is submitted in the guise of "objective truth." This is irresponsible science, because it offers a set of incomplete images lacking a consumer warning that there is something more that has been ignored.

Critical ethnographers recognize that theories and concepts are only partial. Therefore, they warn readers that the constructs that guide inquiry are simply "living signposts" denoting the status of a particular mode of inquiry at a particular time. Critical thinking that challenges accepted images and tweaks the conscience into intellectual reexamination and social action embodies a struggle over ideas, metaphors, policies, and behavior. Critical ethnography is intellectually responsible because it provides a consumer warning while attempting to refine its product, and because its product revitalizes our conceptual and methodological frameworks and their applicability to both research and social action.

A third reason for engaging in critical research lies in its emancipatory potential to free us from existing forms of cultural domination. The project of science is neither disinterested nor detached. The ultimate goal is to provide understandings that can be applied to the world around us. Science in action can change material artifacts, ideas, or symbols. Science for its own sake, or "private science," is a neurotic enterprise, because without some recognition of its relationship to something external to the research setting, it becomes hopelessly self-indulgent.

Science functions to free us from ignorance, and critical science is emancipatory to the extent that it requires continually questioning the limits of our certitude. Habermas (1971) contends that the only knowledge that can truly orient action is knowledge that frees itself from mere human interests and takes on a "theoretical attitude." A theoretical attitude is one that recognizes the sources and the consequences of the power of ideology and language in producing what we call truth.

Approaches to science contain a *cognitive interest* that provides the organizing framework for the questions we ask, how we ask them, and what we do with the answers. So-called objectivist science, typified by positivism, is guided by a cognitive interest of predictability and control. Hermeneutic science, characterized by interpretive social science (including ethnography), aims to understand the world interpretively by deciphering meanings. Critical science is guided by the cognitive interest of emancipating us from the unnecessary forms of social domination by identifying and challenging them. By uncovering what is normally concealed, critical ethnography contributes to the emancipatory project that conventional science fails.

Finally, drawing from a long tradition of moral philosophy, ethnographers should adopt a critical stance because they have an ethical obligation to do so. The premise here is that it is ultimately better to be nice than not nice, and perpetuating social conditions that are not nice is simply not nice. Critical science proceeds from the assumption that we can identify and rank social values: Some people should not unfairly benefit at the expense of others, nonviolence is preferable to violence, and cultural systems that inhibit the development of our full human potential—whatever it might be—should be altered so that they do not. The ontology of critical thought includes a conception, albeit vague, that there is something better, and that the goal of knowledge should include working toward it. There is always room for honest intellectual disagreement over what constitutes "something better," but even these debates, for critical scholars, are part of the process of knowledge production.

Conclusion

Fred Davis (1974) reputedly teaches his graduate methods students by asking, "What's the story, Ritchie?" Data are subject to numerous interpretations, and the "story" we use to organize and transfer those interpretations to others are the various theories to which we cling. One problem with most sociological stories is the adherence to the primacy of professional technique and authority. The story of critical ethnographers is directed toward challenging this primacy.

If critical ethnography is about anything, it is about freedom from social repression and a vision of a better society. Research helps identify what oppresses and how it can be altered. It requires that we understand our subjects, our culture, and above all ourselves as a way of dispelling myths and misconceptions that format social structures and behavior. By invoking our wild side, we are not seeking an idyllic world or utopian dream. Instead, critical ethnographers challenge comfortable, but repressive, cultural definitions and offer an invitation to engage in social change. When done poorly, critical ethnography rarely rises beyond exhortation and political rhetoric. But when done with subtlety and adherence to the data, it becomes a powerful means both to understand other cultures and to think about our own in new ways. When we accomplish this, we also gain the potential to transform both ourselves and the world around us in small but perceptible ways. Reversing Sumner's (1883, pp. 121-122) admonition that minding one's own business is a virtue, critical ethnographers invite us to break the chalk instead.

EPILOGUE

The conclusion of any book silences. The author has staked a claim to authority, and no opportunity exists for readers to challenge the author directly. There is no means to clarify or debate the text's dialogue. A "critical" volume is no less susceptible to this silence than others. The irony is not lost that a text that incites subverting the hierarchy of authority can do so safely because you, the reader, remain at a comfortable distance.

In a short volume, violence occurs as complex ideas are crushed into allocated space. Some ideas are simplified and others ignored. Nuances are dismissed, bodies of literature are summarized too quickly, and examples that are perfectly clear to an author do not translate into equally clear images for the reader.

How can the contradiction between a text's authority and the inability to interrogate the author be overcome? With the accessibility of the electronic communication matrix offered by Bitnet, Internet, and other channels, students, instructors, and researchers can readily communicate with each other. I suggest that those who wish to do so, either as individuals or as a class, take advantage of the computer networking available at most schools. I am willing to continue "writing" this volume by engaging in dialogue, debate, or general discussion with any who wish to contact me at tk0jut1@mvs.cso.niu.edu or jthomas@well.sf.ca.us. Developing ideas does not occur in a vacuum, and ongoing challenges to an author are integral to the critical process. I invite readers to transform this ending critically into a prologue for a new beginning.

REFERENCES

Adler, P. A., & Adler, P. (1987). *Membership roles in field research.* Newbury Park, CA: Sage.

Agar, M. H. (1980, April). Getting better quality stuff: Methodological competition in an interdisciplinary niche. *Urban Life, 9,* 24-50.

Agar, M. H. (1982, December). Toward an ethnographic language. *American Anthropologist, 84,* 779-795.

Agar, M. H. (1986). *Speaking of ethnography.* Beverly Hills, CA: Sage.

Alinsky, S. D. (1969). *Reveille for radicals.* New York: Vintage.

Andersen, M. L. (1981, October). Corporate wives: Longing for liberation or satisfied with the status quo? *Urban Life, 19,* 311-327.

Anderson, D. J. (1986). *Curbing the abuses of inmates litigation.* College Park, MD: American Correctional Association.

Anderson, N. (1923). *The hobo.* Chicago: University of Chicago Press.

Antonio, R. J. (1991, Fall). Postmodern storytelling versus pragmatic truth-seeking: The discursive bases of social theory. *Sociological Theory, 9,* 154-163.

Argyris, C., & Schon, D. A. (1991). Participatory action research and action science compared. In W. F. Whyte (Ed.), *Participatory action research* (pp. 85-96). Newbury Park, CA: Sage.

Aronowitz, S., & Giroux, H. A. (1991). *Postmodern education: Politics, culture, and social criticism.* Minneapolis: University of Minnesota Press.

Balbus, I. D. (1977). *The dialectics of legal repression: Black rebels before the American courts.* New Brunswick, NJ: Transaction Books.

Ball, D. W. (1967, Winter). An abortion clinic ethnography. *Social Problems, 14,* 293-301.

Ball, R. A., & Lilly, J. R. (1982, June). The menace of margarine: The rise and fall of a social problem. *Social Problems, 29,* 488-498.

73

Barthes, R. (1983). *Elements of semiology.* New York: Hill and Wang.

Becker, H. S. (1963). *Outsiders: Studies in the sociology of deviance.* New York: Free Press.

Becker, H. S. (1967, Winter). Whose side are we on? *Social Problems, 14,* 239-247.

Beisel, N. (1990, February). Class, culture, and campaigns against vice. *American Sociological Review, 55,* 44-62.

Bell, D. (1976). *The cultural contradictions of capitalism.* New York: Basic Books.

Berger, P. L., & Luckmann, T. (1967). *The social construction of reality: A treatise in the sociology of knowledge.* Garden City, NY: Anchor.

Bergesen, A. J. (1977, April). Political witch hunts: The sacred and the subversive in cross-national perspective. *American Sociological Review, 42,* 220-233.

Berman, R. (1990, Fall). Troping to Pretoria: The rise and fall of deconstruction. *Telos, 85,* 4-16.

Block, M. (1983). *Marxism and anthropology: The history of a relationship.* Oxford, UK: Clarendon.

Block, M. (1989). *Ritual, history and power: Select papers in anthropology.* London: Athlone.

Bok, S. (1983). *Secrets: On the ethics of concealment and revelation.* New York: Pantheon.

Bourdieu, P. (1977). *Outline of a theory of practice.* New York: Cambridge University Press.

Bourdieu, P. (1984). *Distinction: A social critique of the judgement of taste.* Cambridge, MA: Harvard University Press.

Bourdieu, P. (1991). *Language and symbolic power.* Cambridge, MA: Harvard University Press.

Bourdieu, P., & Passeron, J. (1979). *The inheritors: French students and their relation to culture.* Chicago: University of Chicago Press.

Bowker, L. H. (1977). *Prisoner subcultures.* Lexington, MA: Lexington Books.

Bowler, A., & McBurney, B. (1991, November). Gentrification and the avant-garde in New York's East Village: The good, the bad and the ugly. *Theory, Culture and Society, 8,* 49-77.

Brakel, S. J. (1987). Prison reform litigation: Has the revolution gone too far? *Corrections Today, 49,* 160-168.

Burke, K. (1989). *On symbols and society.* Chicago: University of Chicago Press.

Cahill, S. E. (1989, Fall). Fashioning males and females: Appearance management and the social reproduction of gender. *Symbolic Interaction, 12,* 281-298.

Camus, A. (1955). *The myth of Sisyphus.* New York: Vintage.

Camus, A. (1956). *The rebel: An essay on man in revolt.* New York: Vintage.

Camus, A. (1958). *Caligula and other plays.* New York: Vintage.

Carey, J. T. (1975). *Sociology and public affairs: The Chicago school.* Beverly Hills, CA: Sage.

Castellanos, D. (1985, February). *Schooling in Mexican American communities: Power, policy, and ideology in an international context.* Paper presented at the National Association for Interdisciplinary Ethnic Studies conference, Kansas City.

Cavan, R. S. (1928). *Suicide.* Chicago: University of Chicago Press.

Cavan, S. (1966). *Liquor license: An ethnography of bar behavior.* Chicago: Aldine.

Challiand, G. (1969). *The peasants of North Vietnam.* Harmondsworth, UK: Pelican.

74

Clegg, S. (1975). *Power, rule and domination: A critical and empirical understanding of power in sociological theory and organizational life.* London: Routledge and Kegan Paul.

Clegg, S. (1979). *The theory of power and organization.* London: Routledge and Kegan Paul.

Clifford, J. (1988). *The predicament of culture.* Cambridge, MA: Harvard University Press.

Cobb, S., & Rifkin, J. (1991, Winter). Practice and paradox: Deconstructing neutrality in mediation. *Law and Social Inquiry, 16,* 35-62.

Cohen, S. (1980). *Folk devils and moral panics: The creation of the mods and rockers.* New York: St. Martin's.

Collins, R. (1979). *The credential society: An historical sociology of education and stratification.* New York: Academic Press.

Conly, C. H. (1989). *Organizing for computer crime investigation and prosecution.* Washington, DC: National Institute of Justice.

Cressey, P. G. (1932). *The taxi-dance hall: A sociological study in the commercialized recreation and city life.* Chicago: University of Chicago Press.

Cullum-Swan, B., & Manning, P. K. (1992). *Some ethnographic glimpses of death.* Unpublished manuscript, Michigan State University.

Currie, E. P. (1968, August). Crimes without criminals: Witchcraft and its control in Renaissance Europe. *Law and Society Review, 3,* 7-32.

Davenport, S. (1990). *Empowerment and process: Educating parents as advocates for school reform in Chicago, 1985-1990.* Unpublished doctoral dissertation, Northern Illinois University.

Davis, F. (1974, October). Stories and sociology. *Urban Life, 3,* 310-316.

Davis, F. (1988). Clothing, fashion and the dialectic of identity. In D. R. Maines & C. J. Couch (Eds.), *Communication and social structure* (pp. 23-38). Springfield, IL: Charles C Thomas.

Dearruda, E. (1990). *Illinois Literacy Initiative: The politics of partnership and coalitions within the context of adult literacy programs in Chicago during the 1980s.* Unpublished doctoral dissertation, Northern Illinois University.

Denzin, N. K. (1978). *Sociological methods: A sourcebook.* New York: McGraw-Hill.

Denzin, N. K. (1988, June). "Blue velvet": Postmodern contradictions. *Theory, Culture and Society, 5,* 461-473.

Denzin, N. K. (1989). *Interpretive biography.* Newbury Park, CA: Sage.

Denzin, N. K. (1990a, Fall). The spaces of postmodernism: Reading Plummer on Blumer. *Symbolic Interaction, 13,* 145-160.

Denzin, N. K. (1990b, Fall). Harold and Agnes: A feminist narrative undoing. *Sociology Theory, 8,* 198-216.

Derrida, J. (1976). *Of grammatology.* Baltimore: Johns Hopkins University Press.

Derrida, J. (1978). *Writing and difference.* Chicago: University of Chicago Press.

Derrida, J. (1982). *Margins of philosophy.* Chicago: University of Chicago Press.

Diamond, S. (1971, Spring). The rule of law versus the order of custom. *Social Research, 38,* 42-72.

DiIulio, J. J., Jr. (1987). *Governing prisons: A comparative study of correctional management.* New York: Free Press.

Dilthey, W. (1927). *Der Aufbau der Geschichtlichen Welt in den Geisteswissenschaften: Gesammelte Schriften, vol. 7.* Leipzig: B. G. Teubner.

Douglas, J. D. (1976). *Investigative social research.* Beverly Hills, CA: Sage.

Eco, U. (1979). *A theory of semiotics.* Bloomington: University of Indiana Press.

Edin, K. (1991, November). Surviving the welfare system: How AFDC recipients make ends meet in Chicago. *Social Problems, 38,* 462-474.

Elden, M., & Levin, M. (1991). Cogenerative learning: Bringing participation back into action. In W. F. Whyte (Ed.), *Participatory action research* (pp. 127-142). Newbury Park, CA: Sage.

Erikson, K. T. (1966). *Wayward Puritans: A study in the sociology of deviance.* New York: John Wiley.

Faris, E. (1970). *Chicago sociology: 1920-1932.* Chicago: University of Chicago Press.

Featherstone, M. (1988, June). In pursuit of the postmodern: An introduction. *Theory, Culture and Society, 2,* 195-215.

Fish, S. (1989). *Doing what comes naturally: Change, rhetoric, and the practice of theory in literary and legal studies.* Durham, NC: Duke University Press.

Friedman, M.. (1973). *Problematic rebel: Melville, Dostoievsky, Kafka, Camus.* Chicago: University of Chicago Press.

Friere, P. (1972). *Pedagogy of the oppressed.* New York: Herder and Herder.

Gadamer, H. (1976). *Philosophical hermeneutics.* Berkeley: University of California Press.

Ganguly, K. (1990). Ethnography, representation, and the reproduction of colonialist discourse. In N. K. Denzin (Ed.), *Studies in symbolic interaction: A research journal, vol. 11* (pp. 69-79). Greenwich, CT: JAI.

Geertz, C. (1973). *The interpretion of cultures.* New York: Basic Books.

Geertz, C. (1980, Spring). Blurred genres: The refiguration of social thought. *American Scholar, 49,* 165-179.

Geertz, C. (1988). *Works and lives: The anthropologist as author.* Stanford, CA: Stanford University Press.

Genovese, E. D. (1976). *Roll, Jordan, roll: The world the slaves made.* New York: Vintage.

Girard, R. (1985). *The scapegoat.* Baltimore: Johns Hopkins University Press.

Gladwin, C. H. (1989). *Ethnographic decision tree modeling.* Newbury Park, CA: Sage.

Glaser, B. G., & Strauss, A. L. (1967). *The discovery of grounded theory: Strategies for qualitative research.* New York: Aldine.

Godelier, M. (1972). Structure and contradiction in capital. In R. Blackburn (Ed.), *Ideology in social science: Readings in critical social theory* (pp. 334-368). Suffolk, UK: Fontana/Collins.

Godelier, M. (1978, December). Infrastructures, societies, and history. *Current Anthropology, 19,* 763-771.

Goffman, E. (1959). *The presentation of self in everyday life.* New York: Anchor.

Goffman, E. (1961). *Asylums: Essays on the social situation of mental patients and other inmates.* New York: Anchor.

Goffman, E. (1963). *Encounters: Two studies in the sociology of interaction.* Indianapolis: Bobbs-Merrill.

Goffman, E. (1967). *Interaction ritual: Essays on face-to-face behavior.* New York: Anchor.

Goffman, E. (1979). *Gender advertisements.* New York: Harper and Row.

Goodenough, W. H. (1981). *Culture, language, and society.* Menlo Park, CA: Benjamin/ Cummings.

Goodwin, G. A. (1971, March). On transcending the absurd. *American Journal of Sociology, 76,* 831-846.

Gortz, A. (1968). *Strategy for labor: A radical proposal.* Boston: Beacon.

Gottdiener, M. (1982, July). Disneyland: A utopian urban space. *Urban Life, 11,* 139-162.

Gouldner, A. (1968, May). The sociologist as partisan: Sociology and the welfare state. *American Sociologist, 3,* 103-116.

Gouldner, A. (1970). *The coming crisis of Western sociology.* New York: Basic Books.

Gover, R. (1961). *The one hundred dollar misunderstanding.* New York: Grove.

Habermas, J. (1971). *Knowledge and human interests.* Boston: Beacon.

Habermas, J. (1972). Toward a theory of communicative competence. In H. P. Dreitzel (Ed.), *Recent sociology, no. 2: Patterns of communicative behavior* (pp. 115-148). New York: Macmillan.

Habermas, J. (1979). *Communication and the evolution of society.* Boston: Beacon.

Habermas, J. (1984). *The theory of communicative action, vol. 1: Reason and the rationalization of society.* Boston: Beacon.

Habermas, J. (1987). *The philosophical discourse of modernity: Twelve lectures.* Cambridge: MIT Press.

Hammersley, M. (1990). *Reading ethnographic research: A critical guide.* New York: Longman.

Hammersley, M. (1991). *What's wrong with ethnography?* New York: Routledge.

Harvey, D. H. (1989). *The condition of postmodernity: An enquiry into the origins of cultural change.* Cambridge, MA: Basil Blackwell.

Hawkes, T. (1972). *Metaphor: The critical idiom.* London: Metheun.

Heaney, T. W. (1983). "Hanging on" or "gaining ground": Educating marginal adults. In G. Kasworm (Ed.), *Educational outreach to select adult populations: New directions for continuing education, no. 20* (pp. 53-63). San Francisco: Jossey-Bass.

Hebdige, D. (1982). *Subculture: The meaning of style.* New York: Methuen.

Hoggart, R. (1971). *Only connect: On culture and communication.* London: Chatto and Windus.

Hollinger, R., & Lanza-Kaduce, L. (1988, February). The process of criminalization: The case of computer crime laws. *Criminology, 26,* 101-126.

Horowitz, R. (1982, April). Adult delinquent gangs in a Chicano community: Masked intimacy and marginality. *Urban Life, 11,* 3-26.

Horowitz, R. (1983). *Honor and the American dream: Culture and identity in a Chicano community.* New Brunswick, NJ: Rutgers University Press.

Horowitz, R. (1986, January). Remaining an outsider: Membership as a threat to research rapport. *Urban Life, 14,* 409-430.

Hunt, A. (1991). Postmodernism and critical criminology. In B. MacLean & D. Milovanovic (Eds.), *New directions in critical criminology* (pp. 79-85). Vancouver, BC: Collective Press.

Hymes, D. (Ed.). (1974). *Reinventing anthropology.* New York: Vintage.

Irwin, J. (1987, April). Reflections on ethnography. *Journal of Contemporary Ethnography, 16,* 41-48.

Jacobs, J. (1967, Summer). A phenomenological study of suicide notes. *Social Problems, 15,* 60-72.

Joll, J. (1978). *Antonio Gramsci*. Harmondsworth, UK: Penguin.

Jones, G. S. (1976). *Outcast London: A study in the relationship between classes in Victorian society*. Harmondsworth, UK: Penguin.

Kamuf, P. (1991). *A Derrida reader: Between the blinds*. New York: Columbia University Press.

Kapor, M. (1991, May). Extending the Constitution to American cyberspace. *EFFector Online, 1*(4).

Karlsen, J. I. (1991). Action research as method: Reflections from a program for developing methods and competence. In W. F. Whyte (Ed.), *Participatory research* (pp. 143-158). Newbury Park, CA: Sage.

Katovich, M. A. (1988). Inauthentic identities, suspicion, and honor. In D. Maines & C. Couch (Eds.), *Communication and social structure* (pp. 113-130). Springfield, IL: Charles C Thomas.

Kirk, J., & Miller, M. L. (1986). *Reliability and validity in qualitative research*. Beverly Hills, CA: Sage.

Kirkham, G. (1976). *Signal zero*. Philadelphia: J. B. Lippincott.

Latimer, D. (1984, November/December). Jameson and post-modernism. *New Left Review, 148*, 116-128.

Leal, O. F., & Oliven, R. G. (1988, February). Class interpretations of a soap opera narrative: The case of Brazilian novela "Summer sun." *Theory, Culture and Society, 5*, 81-99.

Lefebvre, H. (1971). *Everyday life in the modern world*. New York: Harper.

Levine, A. G. (1982). *Love Canal: Science, politics, and people*. Lexington, MA: Lexington.

Lincoln, Y. S., & Guba, E. (1985). *Naturalistic inquiry*. Newbury Park, CA: Sage.

Littlefield, A. (1989). The B.I.A. Boarding School: Theories of resistance and reproduction. *Humanity and Society, 13*(4), 428-441.

Lodge, D. (1977). *The modes of modern writing: Metaphor, metonymy, and the typology of modern literature*. Chicago: University of Chicago Press.

Lofland, J. (1987, April). Reflections on a thrice-named journal. *Journal of Contemporary Ethnography, 16*, 25-40.

Lofland, L. H. (1980, October). Reminiscences of classic Chicago: The Blumer-Hughes talk. *Urban Life, 9*, 251-281.

Longhurst, B. (1987, November). Realism, naturalism and television soap opera. *Theory, Culture and Society, 4*, 633-649.

Luckenbill, D. L. (1986, April). Deviant career mobility: The case of male prostitutes. *Social Problems, 33*, 283-296.

Lukacs, G. (1971a). *History and class consciousness: Studies in Marxist dialectics*. London: Merlin.

Lukacs, G. (1971b). *Realism in our time: Literature and the class struggle*. New York: Harper.

Lynd, R. S. (1970). *Knowledge for what? The place of social science in American culture*. Princeton, NJ: Princeton University Press. (Original work published in 1939)

Lyotard, J. (1988a). *The differend: Phrases in dispute*. Minneapolis: University of Minnesota Press.

Lyotard, J. (1988b). *The postmodern condition: A report on knowledge*. Minneapolis: University of Minnesota Press.

78

Lyotard, J., & Thebaud, J. (1985). *Just gaming*. Minneapolis: University of Minnesota Press.

Maguire, P. (1987). *Doing participatory research: A feminist approach*. Amherst, MA: Center for International Education.

Maines, D. R. (1992). Theorizing movement in an urban transportation system by use of the constant comparative method. *Social Science Journal, 29*(3), 283-292.

Mannheim, K. (1938). *Ideology and utopia: An introduction to the sociology of knowledge*. New York: Harcourt, Brace, and World.

Manning, P. K. (1977). *Police work*. Cambridge: MIT Press.

Manning, P. K. (1980). *The narc's game: Organizational and informational limits on drug law enforcement*. Cambridge: MIT Press.

Manning, P. K. (1983). Metaphors of the field: Varieties of organizational discourse. In J. Van Maanen (Ed)., *Qualitative methodology* (pp. 225-245). Newbury Park, CA: Sage.

Manning, P. K. (1986). Signwork. *Human Relations, 39*(4), 283-308.

Manning, P. K. (1987, April). The ethnographic conceit. *Journal of Contemporary Ethnography, 16*, 49-68.

Manning, P. K. (1988). *Symbolic communication: Signifying calls and the police response*. Cambridge: MIT Press.

Manning, P. K. (1989). *Semiotics and postmodernism*. Unpublished manuscript, Michigan State University.

Manning, P. K. (1991). Critical semiotics. In B. D. MacLean & D. Milovanovic, *New directions in critical criminology* (pp. 95-100). Vancouver, BC: Collective Press.

Manning, P. K. (in press-a). The challenges of postmodernism. In J. Van Maanen (Ed.), *Trade secrets*. Newbury Park, CA: Sage.

Manning, P. K. (in press-b). Strands in the postmodernist rope: Ethnographic themes. In N. Denzin (Ed.), *Studies in symbolic interaction, vol. 13*. Greenwich, CT: JAI.

Marcus, G. E., & Fischer, M. M. J. (1986). *Anthropology as cultural critique: An experimental moment in the human sciences*. Chicago: University of Chicago Press.

Marx, G. T. (1988). The maximum security society. *Deviance et Societie, 12*(2), 147-166.

Marx, K. (1974). *The German ideology*. New York: International Publishers. (Original work published 1846)

McBarnet, D. J. (1981). *Conviction: Law, the state and the construction of justice*. London: Macmillan.

McEwen, J. T. (1989). *Dedicated computer crime units*. Washington, DC: National Institute of Justice.

Meyer, G., & Thomas, J. (1990). The baudy world of the byte bandit: A postmodernist interpretation of the computer underground. In F. Schmalleger (Ed.), *Computers in criminal justice* (pp. 31-67). Bristol, IN: Wyndham Hall.

Mills, C. W. (1967). *Power, politics and people: The collected essays of C. Wright Mills*. New York: Oxford University Press.

Mills, C. W. (1970). *The sociological imagination*. New York: Oxford University Press.

Milovanovic, D., & Thomas, J. (1989, February). Overcoming the absurd: Prisoner litigation as primitive rebellion. *Social Problems, 36*, 48-60.

Mueller, C. (1972). Notes on the repression of communicative behavior. In H. P. Dreitzel (Ed.), *Recent sociology, no. 2: Patterns of communicative behavior* (pp. 101-113). New York: Macmillan.

Naples, N. A. (1991, August). Contradictions in the gender subtext of the war on poverty: The community work and resistance of women from low income communities. *Social Problems, 38,* 316-332.

Nelson, C., & Grossberg, L. (Eds.). (1988). *Marxism and the interpretation of culture.* Urbana: University of Illinois Press.

Noblit, G. W., & Hare, R. D. (1988). *Meta-ethnography: Synthesizing qualitative studies.* Newbury Park, CA: Sage.

Park, R. E. (1967). *On social control and collective behavior: Selected papers.* Chicago: University of Chicago Press.

Pepper, S. C. (1948). *World hypotheses: A study in evidence.* Berkeley: University of California Press.

Pfohl, S. (1990, November). Welcome to the parasite cafe: Postmodernity as a social problem. *Social Problems, 37,* 421-442.

Pfohl, S. (1991, Fall). Postmodernity as a social problem: Race, class, gender and the "new world order." *Society for the Study of Social Problems Newsletter, 22,* 9-14.

Pfohl, S., & Gordon, A. (1986, October). Criminological displacements: A sociological deconstruction. *Social Problems, 33,* 94-113.

Plunkett, J. (1971). *Strumpet city.* London: Panther.

Pollner, M. (1991, June). Left of ethnomethodology: The rise and decline of radical reflexivity. *American Sociological Review, 56,* 370-380.

Quant, R. (1967). *Critique: Its nature and function.* Pittsburgh: Duquesne University Press.

Reed, A. W. (1980). Guilt, innocence, and federalism in habeas corpus. *Cornell Law Review, 65*(1), 1123-1147.

Richardson, L. (1991, Fall). Postmodern social theory: Representational practices. *Sociological Theory, 9,* 173-179.

Rickman, H. P. (Ed.). (1961). *Meaning in history: W. Dilthey's thoughts on history and society.* London: Allen and Unwin.

Rubin, H. J. (1987). Community economic development: The role of the applied sociologist. *Journal of Applied Sociology, 4,* 31-45.

Rubin, H. J., & Rubin, I. S. (1991). *Community organizing and development.* New York: Macmillan.

Russell, S. D. (Ed.). (1989). *Ritual, power, and economy: Upland-lowland contrasts in mainland southeast Asia.* Center for Southeast Asian Studies: Northern Illinois University.

Sartre, J. (1947). *The age of reason.* New York: Bantam.

Sartre, J. (1955). *No exit and three other plays.* New York: Vintage.

Saussure, F. de. (1966). *Course in general linguistics.* New York: McGraw-Hill.

Schleiser, K. H. (1974, September). Action anthropology and the southern Cheyenne. *Current Anthropology, 15,* 277-283.

Schroyer, T. (1975). *The critique of domination: The origins and development of critical theory.* Boston: Beacon.

Schutz, A. (1972). *The phenomenology of the social world.* London: Heinemann.

Schwartz, J. (1990, July 2). Hackers of the world, unite! *Newsweek,* pp. 36-37.

Seaton, E. (1987, Summer). Profaned bodies and purloined looks: The prisoner's tattoo and the researcher's gaze. *Journal of Communication Theory, 11,* 17-25.

Seed, J., & Wolff, J. (1984). Class and culture in 19th century Manchester. *Theory, Culture and Society, 2*(2), 38-53.

80

Shaw, C. R., & McKay, H. D. (1929). *Delinquency areas: A study of the geographic distribution of school truants, juvenile delinquents, and adult offenders in Chicago.* Chicago: University of Chicago Press.

Shor, I. (1980). *Critical teaching and everyday life.* Boston: South End.

Smith, G. W. (1990, November). Political activist as ethnographer. *Social Problems, 37,* 629-648.

Spradley, J. P. (1979). *The ethnographic interview.* New York: Holt, Rinehart & Winston.

Sterling, B. (1992). *The hacker crackdown: Law and order on the electronic frontier.* New York: Bantam.

Street, A. F. (1992). *A critical ethnography of clinical nursing practice.* New York: State University of New York Press.

Sumner, W. G. (1883). *What social classes owe to each other.* New York: Harper.

Tandon, R. (1981). Participatory evaluation and research: Main concepts and issues. In W. Fernandes & R. Tandon (Eds.), *Participatory research and evaluation: Experiments in research as a process of liberation* (pp. 15-34). New Delhi: Indian Social Institute.

Tax, S. (1970). The Fox project. In J. A. Clifton (Ed.), *Applied anthropology: Readings in the uses of the science of man* (pp. 106-112). New York: Houghton Mifflin.

Terkel, S. (1974). *Working: People talk about what they do all day and how they feel about what they do.* New York: Pantheon.

Thomas, J. (1980). *The relationship of federal funding to criminology and policing in the social sciences.* Ann Arbor, MI: University Microfilms International.

Thomas, J. (1983, January). Chicago sociology: An introduction. *Urban Life, 11,* 387-395.

Thomas, J. (1988). *Prisoner litigation: The paradox of the jailhouse lawyer.* Totowa, NJ: Rowman and Littlefield.

Thomas, J., & O'Maolchatha, A. (1989, June). Reassessing the critical metaphor: An optimist revisionist view. *Justice Quarterly, 6,* 143-172.

Thomas, J. (1992). The meaning of race in prison culture: Snapshots in black and white. In M. Lynch & E. B. Patterson (Eds.), *Race and criminal justice* (pp. 126-144). New York: Harrow and Heston.

Thomas, J., & Meyer, G. (1990, September). Joe McCarthy in a leisure suit: (Witch) hunting for the computer underground. *Critical Criminologist, 2,* 19-20.

Thomas, J., & Meyer, G. (1991, November). *From disk to discourse: The images of techno-evil.* Paper presented to the American Society of Criminology annual meeting, San Francisco.

Thomas, W. I., & Znaniecki, F. (1927). *The Polish peasant in Europe and America.* Chicago: University of Chicago Press.

Thompson, E. P. (1975). *Whigs and hunters: The origin of the Black Act.* New York: Pantheon.

Thrasher, F. M. (1927). *The gang.* Chicago: University of Chicago Press.

Tressell, Robert. (1954). *The ragged trousered philanthropists.* London: Lawrence and Wishart. (Original work published 1914)

Van Maanen, J. (Ed.). (1983). *Qualitative methodology.* Beverly Hills, CA: Sage.

Van Maanen, J. (1988). *Tales of the field: On writing ethnography.* Chicago: University of Chicago Press.

Van Maanen, J., & Barley, S. (1985). Cultural organization: Fragments of a theory. In P. J. Frost et al., (Eds.), *Organizational culture* (pp. 31-53). Beverly Hills, CA: Sage.

Wagner, D., & Cohen, M. B. (1991, November). The power of the people: Homeless protestors in the aftermath of social movement participation. *Social Problems, 38,* 543-558.

Walton, R. E., & Gaffney, M. E. (1991). Research, action and participation: The merchant shipping case. In W. F. Whyte (Ed.), *Participatory action research* (pp. 99-126). Newbury Park, CA: Sage.

Weber, M. (1946). *From Max Weber* (H. Gerth & C. W. Mills, Eds.). New York: Oxford University Press.

White, H. (1978). *Tropics of discourse: Essays in cultural criticism.* Baltimore: Johns Hopkins University Press.

Whyte, W. F. (1943). *Street corner society: The social structure of an Italian slum.* Chicago: University of Chicago Press.

Whyte, W. F. (1991). *Social theory for action.* Newbury Park, CA: Sage.

Whyte, W. F., Greenwood, D. J., & Lazes, P. (1991). Participatory action research: Through practice to science in social research. In W. F. Whyte (Ed.), *Participatory action research* (pp. 19-55). Newbury Park, CA: Sage.

Williams, B. (1985, October). Owning places and buying time: Class, culture and stalled gentrification. *Urban Life, 14,* 251-273.

Willis, P. E. (1981). *Learning to labor: How working class kids get working class jobs.* New York: Columbia University Press.

Wirth, L. (1928). *The ghetto.* Chicago: University of Chicago Press.

Yablonsky, L. (1969). *The hippie trip.* New York: Pegasus.

Zorbaugh, H. W. (1929). *The gold coast and the slum: A sociological study of Chicago's Near North Side.* Chicago: University of Chicago Press.

ABOUT THE AUTHOR

JIM THOMAS is Professor of Sociology and Criminology at Northern Illinois University. He received his Ph.D. from Michigan State University in 1980. His publications include studies of prisoners, law and ideology, and computer culture. He is sporadically active in prison and legal reform, and is coeditor (with Gordon Meyer) of *Computer underground Digest*. He is currently involved in research on computer underground culture, including "phreaks," "hackers," and "pirates." He can be found roaming about the Internet and can be reached at jthomas@well.sf.ca.us.

Printed in the United States
879800002BA